In the thrill of the
NIGHT

In the thrill of the
NIGHT

Fishing the Michigan Hex

DAN CATAU

Brook Trout
Publishing

New Baltimore, Michigan

Published by
Brook Trout Publishing Co.
P.O. Box 738
New Baltimore, Michigan 48047

Publisher's Cataloging-in-Publication Data
Catau, Dan.
   In the thrill of the night: fishing the michigan hex / Dan Catau –
   New Baltimore, Mich.: Brook Trout Publishing Co.,1999.
      p. ill. cm.
   ISBN 0-9669306-0-6
   1. Fly-fishing. 2. Fly-fishing — Michigan. I. Title.
SH456 .C38   1999   98-89343
799.1'24   dc—21   CIP

Illustrations and cover illustration by Dan Coulston

PROJECT COORDINATION BY JENKINS GROUP, INC.

02 01 00 99 ◆ 5 4 3 2 1

Printed in the United States of America

This book is dedicated to Skip and Gail Madsen, owners of Skip's Sport Shop in Grayling, Michigan; notable riverboat builder, premier trout fisherman and friend, Jay Stephan; my friends, John and Marilyn Stampfly, Al Pretto, John Kennedy, Tim Leck, Eric Swander and John Schneider; and my old Hex fishing buddy, Mike Caswell.

I would also like to recognize all the fisherpersons who put forth time, effort, patience and perseverance in their pursuit of the large Browns on the infamous Au Sable and Manistee Rivers during the famed "Michigan Caddis (Hex) Hatch."

May you be blessed with good health, good fortune and prowess in your search of the ever-so-weary, large Michigan Brown.

A special dedication to my fiancée, Rita, my brother-in-law, Tom, and my daughter, Katherine, with all my love and affection.

SPECIAL DEDICATION

I WOULD ESPECIALLY LIKE TO DEDICATE THIS BOOK TO Kevin Dinsdale, son of my fiancée, Rita. Kevin unexpectedly left us on October 6, 1998, at the young age of thirty-six.

Kevin was an extraordinary man. His subtle and dry sense of humor and his friendly smirk invaded the hearts of everyone he met. A finer, more compassionate, caring and loving man you shall never find. Kevin was always willing to do anything for anyone,  and he never demanded or requested something in return.

During the fourteen years I knew Kevin, I grew to respect, admire and love him very deeply. He has captured a portion of my heart that will eternally be devoted to him. He will always remain a part of my daily thoughts and nightly prayers. My only hope is that one day we will be reunited, to once again share the bond of friendship and love that we once knew.

May God bless you and give you eternal peace.

My everlasting love,
Dan

CONTENTS

Contents

ACKNOWLEDGMENTS

My lovely fiancée, Rita Dinsdale, for her love, time, patience, understanding and words of encouragement while I wrote this book.

My daughter, Kate, for her love and understanding, and for putting up with me when we went to Grayling, Michigan, for vacation — and I spent the evenings fishing.

My brother-in-law, Tom Klena, for his friendship, kindness and fishing companionship over many years.

Al Pretto and John Kennedy, for our Michigan State University days, friendship, years of fishing together and introducing me to fishing the May fly (Hex) hatch back in the fifties.

Skip and Gail Madsen, for their close friendship, knowledge of fly-fishing, fishing camaraderie and providing me with a location in their sports shop to tie flies each summer.

Eric and Steve Swander, for their long-time fishing companionship, sincere friendship and interest in me as a person.

Jack and Missie Millikin, for their friendship and interest in my fly-tying and fly-fishing accomplishments.

Eric Sharp, for his friendship, fishing expertise and several nice articles about my fly-tying and fly-fishing accomplishments.

Orlan (Lucky) Luckstead, for being a good friend, fishing buddy and allowing me to fish the Au Sable on his property.

John and Marilyn Stampfly, for being good friends, always asking how I did fishing and encouraging me to continue.

Robert Clemens, for being a friend, fishing companion and having faith in my flies.

Mike Caswell, for being a friend, dedicated fishing buddy and sharing his knowledge of fly-fishing.

John Schneider and Terry Messerschmidt, for their friendship, fishing companionship and confidence in my flies.

Jack Hankins and son-in-law, Dan, for their fishing knowledge, expertise and friendship.

Jay Stephan, for his friendship, contributions to fly-fishing, riverboat building, expertise in catching fish and sharing of fly patterns.

I would also like to thank:

Ted Stephan, for his friendship and fishing knowledge.

Freddie, Ziggie, Bill and Bob.

All my friends in Grayling, Michigan.

All fly-fisherpersons.

INTRODUCTION

CATCHING A NICE FIFTEEN TO TWENTY-INCH TROUT DURING THE day is an art. It requires the successful completion of several successive prerequisites. Fly-fishing is a learned skill, particularly when you consider the light tackle used, the restrictive quarters of the river, and the cautioned approach and the flawless presentation of the fly that are necessary to attract the elusive, ever-so-weary trout.

Hooking a Big Brown is hard to do, especially in rivers such as the world-renowned Au Sable and Manistee in the Grayling, Michigan area. These rivers are inundated with logjams, tag alders, underwater snags, overhanging growth and the like. It's tough enough hooking the trout, let alone fighting it through numerous obstacles, created by nature and made by individuals, before landing it. What a feat to behold. A task unheralded anywhere!

All accomplished dry fly-fisherpersons are aware of the primary ingredients and techniques required to take nice trout, especially in streams and rivers that are saturated with natural obstructions, diversions and restrictions. A fisherperson must be equipped with the appropriate rod, matching reel and line, proper tippet size, matching fly (flies), and of course waders, net and other sundries.

To prevent spooking a large fish you have to be concerned with your approach and quiet entry into the water. Your position in the water in relationship to the fish is critical. You want to naturally present your fly in a quarterly fashion upriver, to attain a proper float void of drag. The appropriate method to eliminate drag is to mend your line in the opposite direction the fly is floating. This will give you a longer float, by positioning the fly line behind the fly. Doing so delays the current from taking the line downriver faster than the fly, which is the main cause of drag.

Catching trout on a dry fly requires the constant vigilance of properly presenting the fly to a feeding fish until it strikes. Then the fun begins — and lasts — until the fish is either creeled or released, whatever your pleasure.

If you think dry fly-fishing during the day is difficult, try applying these same techniques at night during the May fly (Hex) or the historically called, "Caddis Hatch," on the Au Sable and Manistee Rivers in northern Michigan. Such a task demands extrasensory perception, since you cannot present a fly to a feeding fish by sight due to your impaired vision in the dark of the night. You have to rely totally on your auditory senses to locate feeding fish. It is a learned skill to discern daylight sounds from nighttime sounds, as they differ significantly.

To locate fish you should first look for spots where the current is swiftest, as these are the areas where food is best presented to feeding fish. Trout remain in these feed troughs, where they can pick off many flies with the least amount of effort. Larger fish select the best feed lanes because as they get older they expend less energy, much like we do.

Remember, your entrance into the water and the positioning of yourself to present a fly are of primary importance. You should position yourself so that your cast to the fish is most advantageous and as short as possible. Once you feel that you have located a fish it is advisable that you allow the fish time to establish its feed cycle and rhythm before you present your fly. Typically you can establish its rhythm after three to five feed cycles. Don't cast to the fish the first or second time you hear it feed because your cast may not be accurate enough, which could spook the fish and put it down for the evening. You're dealing with large fish that are experienced, smart, very coy and know exactly what they want.

If you have never fished the May fly Hex hatch at night for large Browns, you are passing up one of the most rewarding challenges ever — catching a large trout under some of the most adverse conditions possible. Specific attributes required for achieving this milestone are patience, perseverance and tenacity, coupled with approach, caution, positioning and proper presentation of the fly. Properly applied in the right perspective these attributes should net you a nice reward — a Big Brown in the sixteen to twenty-plus-inch category.

The elation you feel after catching a large Brown at night can be equated to winning the Stanley Cup, Super Bowl or World Series! It is truly a *Thrill In The Night*. At least, it is to me!

One way to best describe what it's like to fish for large Browns at night during the Hex hatch is to give you a brief synopsis of my experiences on the Au Sable and Manistee Rivers. I'll start by categorizing, in chronological order, the events and timing chart that occur at this particular time of the year.

First, you must be in Grayling, Michigan, at the right time, which is generally the last two weeks in June and the first week in July. This period can fluctuate a week each way depending upon weather conditions. Warmer weather tends to bring the hatch earlier, while colder weather can delay it. Ideal conditions, such as water temperature, air temperature, humidity, etc. play a major role in idealizing the conditions for the Wiggler (large May fly or Hex nymph) to hatch into the adult stage for mating. The hatch on the Manistee River generally runs a little later (about one week), due to cooler water temperatures.

Secondly, you must be ready to begin fishing by 9:45 p.m. each evening. The mating flight of the Hex usually starts at dark, around 10:05 to 10:15 p.m. The number of flight bugs increases for about the first half-hour until it is over. The extent of the flight and the number of flies is also dependent upon the weather conditions for that evening (warm night, cool night, rain, etc.). Quick identification of a mating flight is easily made by looking into the sky at about 9:55 p.m. and watching for May fly flight bugs flying upstream to mate. If you cast your eyes toward the lighter part of the sky these flight bugs can be easily seen, as some of the flies range in size from 1 to 11/2-inches in length and look like miniature B-52's as the swarm continues to get larger and larger.

Once you have established that a flight is in progress, it now becomes important for you to listen for feeding fish. As the flight draws to a close, large, dying, mating May flies, called Spinners or Spents, will begin hitting the water. They then flow with the current along the feed troughs, passing over the fish that are waiting to feed on them. As the fish begin to feed you want to remember to position yourself in the water at a location that affords you the most advantageous cast, so that your fly floats naturally over the feeding fish. Try not to create wakes or any other disturbance, as these can spook large fish and cause them to stop feeding for the evening.

After the flight is over and you've caught several fish (optimistically speaking) you might think that your fishing is over for the evening. Not so. Now comes the serious part of the evening, when you should begin surveying the water for newly hatched May flies, called Duns.

Weather and other conditions permitting, the Duns will emerge from the muck (Wiggler beds) and rise to the surface to discard their wing casings. Once hatched, Duns remain on the water's surface until their wings are dry enough for them to fly. After taking flight, they come to rest in the trees. After remaining in the trees for twenty-four to seventy-two hours, they become flight bugs and fly upstream to mate. This cycle continues each evening for the next three to four weeks or as long as weather conditions permit.

Hatchers, or Duns, can easily be distinguished from Spinners by their wings, which are upright above the water (imagine small sailboats). Spinners remain on the water's surface, spinning around until they die, as their name indicates.

You can identify if a hatch has occurred or is occurring by looking for certain signs, such as Wiggler casings (called shucks) on the water's surface, especially near muck beds, where they tend to gather. You can also look in logjams or other obstructions in the water where casings may have become lodged.

With regard to preference, I am of the opinion that Big Browns prefer Hatchers to Spinners, because Hatchers, which are larger and juicier than Spinners, present a much livelier and tastier meal.

The hatch can start anytime during the evening or early morning hours. It can last fifteen minutes or as long as five hours. Like the flight, the hatch is also dependent upon weather conditions.

Experience and years of research and development have taught me that a water temperature of 66 to 68-plus degrees Fahrenheit and an ambient temperature of 55 to 60-plus degrees Fahrenheit are ideal. Again these conditions will determine the length and size of the hatch for that evening or day.

Yes, I've seen hatches occur during the day for long periods, if conditions are right. I've seen some Spinner falls as early as 9:30 p.m., but never during the day. The earlier the Spinner falls occur the more difficult it is to take fish, because you are not shielded by the darkness of night. Your figure, large leader and fly may become a liability and limit your effectiveness. Therefore, hope for Spinner falls after 10:00 p.m.

In any event, it is in your best interest to remain in the water until the Spinner falls and hatch are long finished. This is especially true if you are in pursuit of Big Browns, which can be caught anywhere from 10:30 p.m. until three, four or five a.m. I'm not joking. I've done it! The latest or earliest, whatever your fancy, I've caught a Big Brown was at four a.m. This is when patience becomes a virtue and perseverance becomes a necessity, since you must continually present your fly until the long-anticipated strike occurs, if it does.

To enhance your chances of bagging a large trout, I would like to remind you not to become impatient. You don't want to cast your fly to a feeding fish before you have properly located it, selected your most advantageous position and have allowed the fish to establish its natural feed cycle and pattern. Anything short of this may send you home empty-handed.

If you come upon a cruiser, a feeding fish that is picking up flies at several different locations, it is especially important that you allow the fish to establish its pattern — before you cast your fly. The challenge for you has now been increased because of the trout's movement. In fact, sometimes cruisers can be mistaken for two or three feeding fish. I have made this mistake before and not caught anything.

A general habit is for a cruiser to feed in two or three different locations in a triangular pattern. If you hear a fish feed at the #1 location, count to ten and toss the fly above the #2 location. If you're not successful, count to ten again and toss the fly above the #3 location. Continue to repeat this approach until the fish strikes — if you are so lucky.

To be successful at hooking a cruiser, you must keep a constant and vigilant eye and ear toward the trout's feeding habits. Cruisers are extremely difficult to catch in comparison to a fish that feeds in one location. Cruisers may change their pattern at a moment's notice, either moving further upstream, further downstream, sideways, etc. Sometimes I think the fish is trying to avoid your fly, for one reason or another. When this happens, the best thing for you to do is to drop back, let the fish rest for five minutes or so, regroup and try again. If this fails, fall back and punt.

This is the only advice I can give you. After forty years of fishing the Hex hatch, I've not quite figured out why this happens. Maybe this year I'll find the answer. If I do, you can rest assured I will tell you.

Remember, the necessary ingredients to hooking a Big Brown during the Hex hatch are: your ability to read the water to discern where a large trout may be lurking, a cautioned approach and entry into the water, patience in waiting out the flight and hatch, and a flawless presentation of your fly. Apply these skills and I'm sure your success in landing trout will steadily improve.

Good luck and good fortune in your pursuit of Big Browns.

Chapter 1

FLY IDENTIFICATION AND CLASSIFICATION

ONE OF THE FIRST STEPS YOU SHOULD TAKE BEFORE FISHING THE Michigan Hex hatch is to acquire a basic knowledge of the natural flies that are a trout's main diet. This chapter provides a quick and basic reference on the identification and classification of the natural flies and various insects found in the rivers and streams throughout Michigan. I extrapolated this information from several complex and comprehensive publications (see Bibliography).

There are four main orders of flies that make up a trout's diet. They are:

1. May flies (Drakes) - by far the largest class

2. Stone flies

3. Caddis flies

4. Miscellaneous flies
    A. Dobson
    B. Dragon
    C. Alder
    D. Etc.

The flies listed above emulate from the rivers and streams of Northern Michigan. These flies comprise about ninety percent of a trout's diet. Trout will eat these flies either as larvae, nymph and pupa, emergers, and adults. Some examples of the larvae, pupa and nymph stages of these flies, along with their artificial fly synonyms, follow:

Actual Fly	**Artificial Fly Synonym**
1. Large May Fly (Hex)	Wiggler, Spring Wiggler
2. Drakes	Lt. and Dk. Hendrickson Nymph, Lt. and Dk. Cahill Nymph, Quill Gordon, Brown Drake, Hares Ear, Bluewing Olive, Etc. Nymphs
3. Stone Flies	Ted's Stone Fly Nymph, Montana Stone, Giant Black and Yellow Stone Fly Nymphs, Little Brown and Yellow Stone Fly Nymphs
4. Caddis Flies	Caddis larvae and pupa, Elk Hair Caddis (distinguished by casing usually built around them)
5. Miscellaneous Flies	Dragon Fly, Dragon Fly Nymph

This book concentrates on the largest of the flies, the Michigan May fly (Hexagenia Limbata), commonly known as the Hex. May flies grow as long as 1 1/2-inches or more. The larva of the Hex is the Wiggler. Wigglers can be found in the muck beds of streams, rivers and lakes in Michigan. Wigglers wander around in the muck for a period of up to three years, until they hatch into adult May flies. As they hatch, perform their mating ritual and flight, die and fall to the water's surface, May flies become one of the major sources of food for trout.

Female Hexes deposit their eggs by thumping their rear abdomens on the water before they die. Their whole purpose in life is to provide an abundance of high protein food for trout and other fish in a short period of time (approximately three to four weeks). An interesting note is that during their transformation from a Wiggler to an adult fly, Hexes lose their mouths and ability to eat. This accounts for their short life span (only twenty-four to seventy-two hours) as adult flies.

In Michigan, the commonly called "Fish Fly Hatch" in Algonac, New Baltimore, Port Huron, etc. is nothing more than the Michigan May fly or Hex. Other misnomers, such as "Soldier Fly" or "Caddis," have been attached to the Michigan Hex, the latter of which accounts for the term "Caddis Hatch" applied to northern Michigan Hex hatches on streams and rivers.

Let's now take a look at some of the distinguishing characteristics of these four orders of flies:

May Flies (Drakes)
Order: Ephemeroptera

The largest May fly is the Hexagenia Limbata, otherwise known as the Michigan Hex. The smallest May fly is the Tricorythodes (Tricos). Hook sizes range from 4-63x to a #24 and #26 regular.

I.   **Distinguishing Characteristics**

   A.   Two short antennae projecting from the head
   B.   Compound eye
   C.   Either two or three tails, usually long
   D.   Four upright wings, two large and two small
   E.   Segmented full body
   F.   Wings have a coastal margin, stigmatic area, apex, outer margin, rear margin and marginal intercalaries
   G.   Body is usually curved upward
   H.   Front legs are jointed and have a femur, tibia, tarsus and tarsal claws

II. Common Names and Colors of May Flies

A. Hex: yellow body with brown segments, slate-colored wings

B. Brown Drake: dark brown body and wings

C. Gray Drake: gray body and wings

D. Hendrickson (light and dark): brown and blue dun body and wings

E. Ginger Quill: light ginger and tan body and wings

F. Quill Gordon: quill body, wood duck wings and light. blue

G. Mahogany Drake: mahogany body and wings

H. Blue Winged Olive: olive body and blue wings

I. Tricorythode: black body and white wings

STONE FLIES
ORDER: PLECOPTERA

These flies play a major role in a trout's diet, especially in their nymph and adult stages early in the season (May and June).

I. Distinguishing Characteristics

A. Fully-winged and mottled in general

B. Four wings that are folded and held flat over the abdomen when at rest

C. Some have flightless short wings and a few are wingless

D. Fairly long antennae projecting from head

E. Most have fairly long tails; some are tailless

F. Segmented head

G. Pincers on head

H. Large eyes on side of head

I. Jointed legs with suction cup-like ends

II. **Common Names and Colors of Stone Flies**

   A. Yellow Stone: small (all yellow) summer fly

   B. Black Stone: small (all black) fall and winter fly

   C. Giant Black: large (all black) western fly

   D. Giant Yellow: large (all yellow) western fly

   E. Golden Stone: golden colored

   F. Early Brown Stone: medium (all brown)

   G. Green Stone: medium (all green)

CADDIS FLIES
ORDER: TRICHOPTERA

These flies provide an abundance of food for trout in their pupa and larvae stages, as they crawl along the bottoms of streams and rivers, in their home-built casings made of pebbles, clay, wood, etc. A common nickname is Stick worm or Stick Caddis.

I. **Distinguishing Characteristics**

   A. Superficial resemblance to moths

   B. Long, thread-like antennae

   C. No tails

   D. At rest the wings are folded over the back like a tent

   E. Four wings

   F. Expanded, the hind wings are broader than the fore wings

   G. In most species the wings are covered with tiny, hair-like scales

   H. Vary widely in size and color, most Caddis flies are rather drab in appearance

II. **Common Names and Colors of Caddis Flies**

   A. Sedge: gray in color

B. Caddis (most common): large, dark gray or dark brown, black veined, elongated wings

C. Black Dancer: black Caddis fly with enormously long antennae

D. White Miller: white to grayish-white, long antennae

MISCELLANEOUS FLIES
ENCOMPASSES ALL OTHER CATEGORIES

I.   **Distinguishing Characteristics**

Too numerous and varied to specify since this encompasses all other categories of flies not covered in the previous three orders.

II.   **Common Names and Colors of Miscellaneous Flies**

A. Dragon Fly: multi-colored

B. Alder Fly: multi-colored

C. Dobson Fly: multi-colored

D. Damsel Fly: multi-colored

Chapter 2

REQUIRED
NIGHT FISHING EQUIPMENT

BEFORE YOU VENTURE FORTH TO FISH THE HEX HATCH YOU should develop an itemized list of equipment and clothing to take to your favorite spot in the river. If you don't prepare a list, you might arrive at the river and discover that you forgot an important item, such as your rod. By the time you go back home and return to the river the flight and hatch could be over. What a bummer! This could have been the night that you caught your biggest fish or maybe broken a state record. Who knows? Anything is possible — so plan well.

After fishing the Michigan Hex for forty years, I've compiled the following list of items that are required for fishing the Au Sable and Manistee rivers. The items below are not necessarily in order of priority — but they are all important.

1. **Rod** - The best rods are 7 1/2 to 8 1/2-footers, either bamboo, fiberglass or graphite. I prefer graphite because of its light weight and sensitivity. Use whatever type rod you prefer. Also, you might consider leaving a spare rod in your trunk, as I do.

2. **Reel** - The reel you choose can either be an automatic, single or double-action crank type. I prefer the latter because I hand strip my fish until it's netted. I don't fight them off the reel. My experience with automatic reels hasn't been favorable. I've had the spring freeze or break. The maintenance on a single or double-action is a lot less. You may want to carry a spare reel with you, equipped with line, backing and tippet, in case anything happens to the reel you are using.

3. **Fly Line** - Choose either a #6 or #7 weight forward or double-tapered floating fly line. Look for the following letter and number sequence on the fly line box: WF6F, WF7F, DT6F, or DT7F. I prefer a weight forward #6 or #7 because the extra weight thrust forward makes it easier to cast larger Hex flies. In any respect, you should select a good line, as this is one of the main elements in properly presenting your fly and keeping it afloat.

    Cheap lines have a tendency to check and crack easily, take in water quicker and sink faster than better lines. Your line should be dried and cleaned after each night's fishing to ensure its ability to float the next time it is used. Use fly line cleaner, which usually comes with the line, to clean your line. The last thing you want is for your fly line to sink.

    Another consideration is to back your fly line with approximately fifty yards of 15 to 20 lb. Monofilament. This extra backing will permit a large fish to make long runs without breaking or taking all of your line off the reel.

4. **Tippet Material** - Use a 7-foot to 9-foot tippet of 0X, 1X, 2X or 3X material (equates to 12, 10, 8 or 6 lb. test depending on the manufacturer) or you can use 6, 8 or 10 lb. test tippet straight. I've used all of these very effectively. Some

manufacturers of good tippet material are Maxima, Berkeley, Aeon and Gladding. There are others who manufacture comparable quality and micrometer size. Select your preference.

There are several methods used to attach both your tippet and backing to your fly line. You can use the historic nail knot or double loop, splice the tippet and backing into your fly line, or use the plastic bulb or little barbed eyelets which are inserted into the core of the fly line. I like the metal eyelets because they make it easier if a quick change is required at either end of the fly line. Plus, the eyelets flow easier through the guides.

Make sure that when you insert the barbed eyelets into the core of the line they don't pierce through the fly line. This could create a weak spot in the fly line, causing it to break if you have a large fish on your hook. You don't want all of your effort to be for naught at this point and time in the game.

To be better prepared it would behoove you to tie a couple of extra tippets with flies attached (one Hatcher and one Spinner). This way if you lose your fly or complete tippet, you can make a quick and easy change without belaboring the point. The more time your fly spends on the water, the greater your chances are of catching fish. You don't want to waste precious time tying on flies or tippets when fish are feeding around you. The extra tippets with flies attached can be stored safely in your fly vest.

5. **Waders** - Wear either chest high boot type or stocking foot waders with a boot. I prefer chest high, insulated boot waders, just in case the weather cools during the evening.

I suggest you avoid wearing hip boots, as they may not be

high enough for the depth of water you fish. Felt bottoms are not necessary because you will mainly be wading on sandy bottoms. Don't forget your suspenders!

6. **Fly Vest** - Vests are typically three-quarters or full length, whatever your pleasure. Just make sure the vest you choose has ample storage pockets for your sundries.

7. **Warm Clothing** - This is important because of the length of time you may be spending in the cool water during the evening. I usually wear warm socks and pants, a long-sleeved wool shirt, with a jacket and my fly vest over the jacket. You should bring a hat to keep mosquitoes and black flies off of your head and neck. If it stays warm you can always shed clothes. It is easier to remove layers than to put on more clothes to keep warm, especially if you don't have them with you.

8. **Insect Repellent** - I prefer Muskol because it is 100 percent Deet. Bring whatever repellent you prefer — just remember it.

9. **Flashlights** - I use a Mag-lite because I can easily adjust the beam. You can choose to use a regular two-cell flashlight, Flex-light, Mag-lite, whatever. I also carry a spare flashlight, just in case the first Mag-lite should go out for any reason. Additionally, make sure your flashlight is attached to the top of your vest by some means, to avoid dropping it into the river.

10. **Other important items** - Bring enough flies, dry fly floatant, clippers, snippers, net, forceps, etc. My preference for a dry fly floatant has always been Mucilin, a white, pasty material that is made in England. Aside from lasting longer, you can put some on your fly vest to avoid hunting for it every time you need it. Use whatever floatant you

like. As long as you are happy with the job your floatant does in keeping your fly afloat, it doesn't matter if it is a paste, silicone spray or silicone liquid. The last thing you need is a sinking fly, especially during the peak of the hatch. (Later on in the book I explain my fly pattern for the Hex, which has become one of the most effective flies used on the Au Sable and Manistee rivers for the past thirty-five years.)

Chapter 3

MANISTEE RIVER FISHING EXPERIENCES

I WAS BLESSED WITH THE GOOD FORTUNE OF FISHING THE HEX hatch — in its entirety — for four straight years. From April 1981 to October 1984 I owned the King Trout Ranch, located on the Manistee River, three miles upstream from the CCC Bridge Campground (about twenty minutes from Grayling). I will cherish these years for the rest of my life, as they provided me with the most challenging and rewarding fishing experiences in my forty years of fly-fishing. Many nights, after I finished my chores around the Ranch, I would don my fishing wardrobe and proceed to one of my favorite spots on the Manistee River to anxiously await the arrival of the May fly flight and hatch. I always harbored encouraging thoughts of catching a large Brown or two.

Several times my hopes became reality, as I ended an evening of fishing with two or three Browns ranging from 17 to 20-inches and weighing 2 1/2 to 3 1/2 pounds. This was not an everyday occurrence; in fact, quite the contrary. It was rare when I would hook and land several large fish in one evening.

There were nights when I located large fish and proceeded to

MANISTEE RIVER LOCATIONS

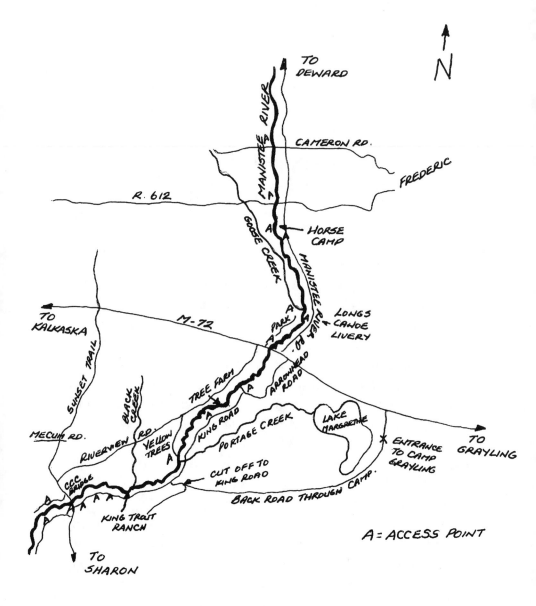

cast my fly, cast my fly and cast and cast and cast — only to depart the river empty-handed. Some nights I wouldn't even get a strike. Nights like that have to be accepted, along with the good times. I chalked them up to the "gaining experience" category, as I reminded myself that the pleasure of fly-fishing wasn't only about how many fish I caught or how big they were.

The completeness of fishing the Hex hatch is being able to wade through the river and cast to feeding fish, in constant anticipation of that one strike and potential run for your life. My love of fly-fishing, nature's many endowments and the serenity of the sport are what I enjoy most. They are what keep me coming back year after year.

I will now take you back in time to relive some of my most memorable experiences fishing the Hex on the Manistee River . . .

🦟   🦟   🦟

As I RECALL, IT WAS ABOUT 9:00 P.M. ON JUNE 27, 1984. I HAD COMpleted my chores around the Ranch and knew that the Hex hatch had started two days earlier. It was a nice warm evening of about 65 degrees. The sun was beginning to nestle behind the towering pines, before it settled for the evening. Its bright orange-reddish color cast a brilliant shine upon the Manistee. It was an ideal night for the Hex. I decided to try my hand at catching some Browns.

Most of the fishermen that were staying at the Ranch had left the premises in search of large Browns at their favorite spots up and down the Manistee. This meant that the river in front of the Ranch was wide open for me to fish.

I donned my usual fly-fishing paraphernalia and got into the river about 9:30 p.m. I walked upstream a couple of bends to a large logjam that held about eight to nine feet of water and offered considerable cover. This was a prime location for a large fish as the current created an excellent feed trough by washing Spinners and Hatchers tight to the jam.

At about 9:50 p.m. I looked up into the sky to see if I could detect the first indications of a mating flight. After perusing the sky and water surface for ten minutes I began to pick out a few flight bugs flying upstream about fifteen feet above the water's surface. The sight of these Hexes automatically began to circulate adrenaline into my system, causing my heart to beat harder and harder in anticipation of hearing the first feeding fish.

After about five minutes I heard a familiar sound. A fish was feeding approximately twenty yards upriver on my side, against the bank near some overhanging tag alders. I slowly made my way across the river to a more advantageous location, so I could better identify its location.

About thirty seconds later, the fish fed again. It was directly across river from where I was now standing. I positioned myself where I felt I could make the best cast with minimal drag. I waited. The fish fed a third time. I now knew exactly where it was. I would let it feed one more time before casting my fly. It did so.

I stripped off what I felt was an appropriate length of line from my reel and cast my fly some ten feet above the fish. As soon as my fly hit the water, I mended my line to accomplish the desired float. As my fly floated over the feeding fish, I prepared for the strike — but nothing happened. I gently picked my fly off the water, false cast twice and proceeded to cast in the same location. Again, nothing happened. My next three casts had the same results.

On my next cast, as my fly floated over the fish, I heard the sound I had been waiting for all night. I picked up my rod tip, set the hook and the fish was on. It made several runs up and down the river, heading toward tag alders, other snags and a logjam, in hopes of tangling me up and breaking loose.

After steering it away from all the obstructions, I finally turned the fish and brought it toward me. Slowly I hand stripped the line, ready to let loose at a moment's notice should it decide to make another run. I placed my net in the water and landed the fish. The battle was over. She was a decent, chunky Brown measuring 17 1/2 inches and weighing approximately 2 1/2 pounds.

I had bagged my first fish of the evening. My first hurdle was surmounted. My next step was to return back downstream to my initial location in front of the jam, where I knew another big fish was lurking. Fifteen minutes went by. Everything remained calm.

By this time the Spinner fall was ending and I was beginning to wonder if the evening would produce any further activity. I decided to wait in front of the jam for about half an hour and then wade downstream to see if I could pick up any stragglers that might still be feeding. Ten minutes passed. I thought I heard a fish feeding downstream approximately thirty to forty yards and across river. Knowing the river, I suspected that it was feeding near a small log and some overhanging tag alders near a point in the river before a large bend.

As I made my way downriver, it fed again. It was close to the bank and under the tag alders, exactly where I suspected it might be. Once again I positioned myself at the best vantage point to successfully present my fly. My second cast took the fish. It made its runs with more authority and seemed a little stronger than the first fish. I fought it for a few minutes and brought it to rest in my net. It was a hefty 18 1/2-inch male, and probably weighed close to 3 pounds. Even if I didn't catch another fish, my evening would be complete. Two nice trout was a good evening's fishing.

The activity began to slow down considerably as the Spinner fall drew to a close. It was 11:30 p.m. Being the persistent individual that I am, I once again waded back upstream to camp in front of the large jam. About halfway up I heard a slurp in the general vicinity of the jam.. I continued upriver only to notice several Hatchers floating down. I knew that if the Hatchers decided to pop, this surely would entice a Big Brown into a feeding frenzy.

As I returned to my original position in front of the jam, I heard a big slurp. I turned slightly to locate the fish and saw a large ring with a bubble the size of a baseball floating downriver. This is what I had been waiting for all evening: Moby Dick. Experience told me that from the size of the ring and the water that moved I was not dealing with a piker. This fish had to be in the twenty-plus-inch category.

I turned my back on the fish and shined my flashlight upstream on a Wiggler bed located about thirty feet above the jam. Lo and behold, the Hatchers were beginning to float down the river. I remembered that I still had a Spinner on, and that this would not entice this old trout. Anxiously, with my hands shaking terribly, I made three feeble attempts to tie on a Hatcher. The fourth try proved to be successful. During a span of about one-and-half-minutes, the fish fed two more times, each time more vigorously than before. It was definitely in a voracious feed cycle. I didn't like my position in relationship to the fish, so I cautiously moved upstream a few more feet. I surely didn't want to create any disturbances in the water for fear that the fish might stop feeding. (I've been in this predicament before with a large fish and put it down with my wake, a lesson never to be forgotten.) The fish continued to feed. I made five or six perfect casts, or so I thought, but to no satisfaction. It continued feeding and ignored my fly.

My next cast presented the fly perfectly. About ten feet into the float my line suddenly stopped. Thinking I was probably hung up on a log I picked the rod tip up. The line didn't budge. I pulled a little harder, still trying to free it — and all hell broke loose. There was a tremendous boil in the water and I knew I had a monster on. The weight and strength told me that much. If I thought I was in a battle with the 17-inch and 18-inch trout earlier, I was now in a full-scale, all out war. The fish, realizing that it was hooked, made a strong, steady run upstream to a point where it began to get into the 20-pound backing on my reel. Just as I began to turn it, the fish decided to come back down as fast as it could, directly at me. My immediate concern was to take up the line quickly, so as not to slack off on the tension I was applying. Could I do it?

Miraculously, I took in the line fast enough as the fish passed me and made a run downstream for about forty feet. From there it made several crisscross runs across the river, constantly attempting to tangle me up in several snags on the bottom. Finally, it came to rest on the bottom, some twenty-five feet downriver. I suspected it was sulking on the bottom, digging its nose in the sand, trying to shake my fly. I couldn't budge it. I knew there was a shallow sand bar directly across on my right, from where it had settled. I figured that if I could wade down to the sand bar I might be able to get the fish off the bottom and beach it. I knew I had no chance of netting it by myself. Oh how I wished that somebody was there to help with the final touches and to finish off the fish. Alas, it was all up to me.

As I waded downriver, constantly retrieving line, I remembered that thumping the butt section of the rod on my palm might get the fish moving again, by telegraphing a vibration to it. I thumped the butt and, much to my surprise, the fish began moving again. I then worked it over the shallow sand bar, reached into the water with my right hand, grabbed its tail and threw it up into the weeds surrounding the bar. The fish began to thrash crazily, so I immediately thrust my 240-pound torso on top of him and buried him in the muck.

It seemed as though an eternity had passed, but the fight only lasted twenty minutes from start to finish. After about ten minutes I regained my senses as my weakness and excitement began to subside. I took a look at the trout I had landed. It was a large, hefty, hooked-jawed male, somewhere in the 24 to 25-inch class. I guessed that he weighed five pounds or more. What a fish! I really wouldn't know how big he was until I got back to the Ranch.

I cut the leader, left the fly in his jaw and put him in my creel.

He was so big that his head and tail stuck up above the creel, even though he was doubled over. I started my journey downriver to where I could get out and return to the Ranch.

On my way downriver I heard two or three other decent fish feeding on Hatchers, but I didn't even consider fishing for them. My psychological and physical condition was not up to par. I was thoroughly exhausted from the war I had just fought — and won.

As I came to the place in the river near the Ranch I climbed out and trotted to the house, yelling for my wife and daughter, who were nicely tucked away in their beds for the evening. They got up to see what the commotion was about. I showed them my grand prize for the evening. They were both stricken with awe in their half-dazed state. Little did I realize that it was 1:30 a.m. I then measured and weighed the fish. It was 24 inches long and weighed a whopping five pounds.

It was surely an occasion I would remember forever. To this day each detail remains clearly embossed in my mind. The fish now sits, motionless, on my wall, reminding me of that very special evening, *In the Thrill of the Night*.

※   ※   ※

ANOTHER MEMORABLE FISHING EXPERIENCE ON THE MANISTEE RIVER is about my good friend, Bud Galbraith. Bud was a retired professional photographer from the Indianapolis area. He was a fly-tying student of mine when I was assigned to a Chrysler plant in Indiana. During this time I also managed an Orvis Fly Shop, which is where I first met Bud. An avid fly-fisherman, Bud expressed his desire to fish the Michigan Hex hatch at some point and time in his life.

In June 1981, after I had purchased the King Trout Ranch and moved to northern Michigan, I heard from Bud. He wanted to come up and spend two months of R&R fishing. Two days later he arrived at the Ranch. We renewed our acquaintance, exchanged fish stories, tied some flies and discussed the Hex hatch. I told Bud that he had come at an excellent time. The hatch was at its peak.

We decided to fish that evening. Since Bud hadn't fished the Hex hatch before, we spent some time reviewing the necessary techniques for night fishing. I decided to act as Bud's guide, confidant and fish locator on our first night out. I would not do any fishing.

Bud came to my house at about 9:30 p.m., ready to go fishing. I suggested that we head downriver a couple of bends, to a spot where I had located three decent fish. I had spotted the fish a month earlier, while I was wading in the river scouting out good locations to fish during the Hex hatch. I hadn't heard of anyone catching any decent fish, so I knew they were still there. (Big Browns select the best feed troughs and usually stay in the same hole until they have to move for one reason or another. And, if they do leave, usually another fish the same size takes their place.)

We proceeded downriver about 9:45 p.m. and settled on a log directly across river from where I had spotted the fish. We would now await the flight bugs.

About fifteen minutes passed, without any activity. We became immersed in conversation. Another fifteen minutes lapsed, and still nothing. Thoroughly engrossed in our conversation by now, we failed to observe if any flight bugs were in the air. This is a cardinal sin, especially since it was now too dark for us to see very well. We stopped talking and began to pay attention to what was happening on the river.

Finally I heard what I thought was a fish feeding. I asked Bud if he had heard it. He responded with a resounding yes, but he didn't know where the noise had come from. I shined my flashlight on the water and saw a few Spinners floating down.

The fish fed again. It appeared to be directly across river some thirty feet. I knew the general location and suspected that it was near a couple of snags in the river and an overhanging cedar. We heard it again. I then pinpointed its location and told Bud exactly where it was and how he should approach it.

We moved down about five feet so Bud could position himself for a better cast and float over the fish. The fish fed again. Bud stripped off about thirty feet of line and cast his fly about fifteen feet above the fish. Nothing happened. Bud cast a second, third and fourth time without any result. On his fifth cast we heard the long awaited slurp. Bud picked up his rod tip, set the hook and the fish was on.

I instructed Bud to keep his rod tip high and to continue applying tension. This way the fish would fight the rod instead of the line, which could easily break. After about two or three runs up and down and across the river the fish came at me. I asked Bud to work it over to me so that I could net it for him. He did and I netted the fish. It was a hefty, 18 1/2-inch female, weighing close to three pounds.

While Bud was fighting the fish I had heard several other fish feeding, one real nice one about twenty-five feet upstream in the middle of the river. We cautiously worked our way upstream along the shore to a position where the fish was a little downstream (about 12 to 14 feet away). We let the fish feed a couple of more times before Bud cast his fly in a quarterly fashion above the fish. His first cast hooked the fish, which made several strong runs and headed for a logjam across the river. Bud steered it away from the jam. The fish then darted back upriver toward some snags. Bud brought it back again. The fish made another good run before it settled on the bottom about ten feet away.

I told Bud to keep his rod high and apply a little more pressure on the line. When he did this the fish took off again and came toward Bud. As before, Bud worked the fish over to me. I netted a second fish for the evening. It was a 19 1/2-inch male, weighing three-plus pounds.

Bud was elated. Between the excitement of hooking two Big Browns and the adrenaline pumping through his system from fighting the fish, Bud said he felt drained. He had never experienced fishing for Big Browns, and he was extremely pleased with his performance. So was I. He was an excellent student. We decided to call it an evening.

As the Spinners became sparser on the water's surface (by this time the air had cooled to about 45 degrees), we waded back upstream to where we could get out and head back to the Ranch. About twenty feet into our wade, another fish fed upstream, apparently eating some straggling Spinners that were falling. I suggested to Bud that he go for it — but he declined. He said that I should try for it. Even though I had not planned to fish that evening, I did not have the will power to keep my line out of the water. To resist the challenge and excitement of fishing for a Big Brown during the hatch is an impossible task, at least for me.

Bud and I cautiously waded upstream to locate the fish. It fed twice more before we located it, about fifteen feet ahead in a log-jam tight to the right bank. We moved slightly up and out toward the middle of the river for a better casting position. I took the fish on my second cast and fought it for a few minutes before it came to rest in my net. It was a nice, 18 1/2-inch, chunky, female.

After this last catch, we saw no evidence of any Hatchers and decided to call it an evening. Although we left the river early, this night would be remembered.

During the next two weeks Bud and I would take several other nice Browns that ranged between 15 and 19 inches. This was a season of Hex fishing we would not forget soon, as it brought much peacefulness and joy to us.

I had looked forward to many more years of fishing with Bud, but we only had two seasons to fish the Hex hatch. Bud unexpectedly became ill and was not able to return in later years. It's a shame that Bud only had two years to fish the Hex hatch, as he had grown to love it so dearly. He died two years later in 1985.

I dedicate this section to my fishing buddy, Bud. I hope that wherever he is, he still enjoys the serenity, tranquility and friendship that we shared that memorable evening in June, fishing the Michigan Hex.

CHARLIE WEAVER IS A GUIDE ON THE MANISTEE AND AU SABLE RIVERS. Years ago he and I shared a first-time experience for Charlie; one that I will always cherish.

Before moving to the Grayling area, Charlie was a special education teacher in Ann Arbor, Michigan. Each summer he would spend three months living in a camper on the Manistee River at the King Trout Ranch. During this period Charlie and I came to be good friends. On many occasions we would tie flies together in my shop and discuss what fly patterns to use on the Manistee and Au Sable Rivers. On a few occasions, as our schedules permitted, we would fish the Hex hatch together.

Charlie was a member of a fishing group called the "Bank Beavers." The Bank Beavers consisted of about twelve men who would gather each year to stalk Big Browns during the Hex hatch. Their base camp was the King Trout Ranch. At night they would disperse, mainly in pairs, to their favorite spots up and down the Manistee. Each of these men had fished the Manistee for at least fifteen years. As a group they had over one hundred and fifty years of Hex hatch experience.

They were premiere Hex fishermen. All of them had bagged Browns in the 19-plus-inch category — everyone except for Charlie, that is. He had never caught a Brown over 17 1/2-inches. Even though he was an excellent fly-fisherman, he was never in the right place at the right time. This is something that has frustrated all Hexers at one time or another.

After a day's work of tying my Hex pattern, Charlie and I decided to go fishing that evening, since the Hex was on. After some capitulation we decided to try our luck upriver, about three miles in front of Earl and Mary Dix's house. They were good neighbors of mine. At this location the river broke out of a narrow chute into a wide, deep stretch and ended with a deep, sweeping bend to the left, before proceeding down. This particular stretch of water afforded an excellent opportunity to catch large trout because it was full of natural cover that provided numerous places for fish to hide and eat.

Just below the chute was a large Wiggler bed where Hatchers would emerge and float downriver until their wings had dried enough for them to leave the water's surface. This was an excellent location for a large trout to gorge itself with lively, tasty Hatchers.

Charlie and I left the ranch at about 9:50 p.m. We arrived at our location at about 10:00 p.m. and positioned ourselves at the tail end of the Wiggler bed to await the Spinner fall and then the hatch. As we looked into the evening sky, that was lit-up by the moon, we detected a few flight bugs in the air, but nothing of any significance. About five minutes passed before we began to hear a few small fish starting to feed. We didn't cast our flies in fear that we would cast our line over a large fish and put it down before it began feeding for the evening.

The Spinner fall lasted about fifteen minutes. We did not take a single fish and we began to think this might be a very unproductive evening. We decided to remove our Spinner pattern and tie on Hatchers, in expectation of a hatch, since the warm, humid air was ideal for such an occurrence.

We sat quietly, enjoying the nocturnal endowments that nature provided. About twenty minutes passed before we heard the first decent fish feed. Wondering if the Hatchers had started, I shined my flashlight directly across the river. We could see a few Hatchers floating down.

The fish fed a second time. I got a general location and thought it was up and across the river, below the Wiggler bed some thirty to forty feet away. We waded a little upstream toward the middle of the river to get a better vantage point. The fish was beginning to establish its rhythm, as it fed for a third time. We now identified its location and Charlie prepared to cast to it. He stripped off about twenty-five feet of line and proceeded to cast. Charlie cast several times but to no avail. The fish was still feeding.

I suggested that he strip off additional line to cast his fly about five feet further. I felt he was a little short on his previous casts and wasn't getting the fly to the fish. Charlie added the extra line and took the fish on his very next cast. "It's a good Brown!" exclaimed Charlie, as the fish fought the hook.

The fish made a substantial run downstream toward us, turned, and then ran back upstream to where it originally lay. It then came back down and went toward the far bank, when suddenly the line stopped. I asked Charlie if he had lost it. "No, but it wasn't moving," he said.

Browns like to head for the bottom of the river to sulk by digging their noses in the sand. This appears to be their last-ditch effort to shake the fly. Knowing this from experience, I told Charlie to thump the butt section of his rod with his palm to get the fish moving again. He thumped the rod and the fish again decided to run. Charlie brought him over to me and I netted him. We took the fish out of the net and measured him. He was 18 3/4-inches long. The biggest Brown Charlie had ever caught. Charlie was elated. I was happy for him, as I had a chance to share this memorable moment of accomplishment.

I asked Charlie what he wanted to do with the trout. Charlie said to release it. I wet my hands, grabbed the fish and walked him around in the water until he could regroup and breathe normally again. We then released him, to swim freely, to eat more flies, and to maybe provide someone else with the same excitement and enjoyment he did for Charlie. We returned to our original position and sat down on the bank to await the possibility of other feeding fish.

Ten minutes went by before we heard the next fish. It was about ten feet below us in the middle of the river. Charlie said, "Your turn, Dan."

"No," I responded.

"I had my fun, now you have yours," he insisted.

Accepting his wishes I stripped off about twenty feet of line and cast to the fish. It took my fly and made several runs before I worked it over to Charlie so he could net it. It was a nice, 17-inch female. Like Charlie, I released the fish, so it could again roam the waters of the Manistee.

Although I have not seen Charlie for the past two years, I suspect that he has since caught several browns in the 20-plus-inch class. He had the makings of an excellent Hex fisherman.

I intend to look Charlie up next June, when I am in Grayling for my two-week stay. Maybe we can fish together again and I'll witness his next biggest fish ever. Who knows what fate has in store for us!

※　※　※

SKIP AND GAIL MADSEN, OWNERS OF SKIP'S SPORT SHOP ARE VERY GOOD friends of mine. They are the center of attraction for my next story about Hex fishing on the Manistee River.

I had driven to Grayling to deliver some flies to Skip. I wanted to let him know that the Hex hatch had started last night at the Ranch and that I had heard several good fish feeding downriver. After hearing the news, Skip and Gail expressed their desire to come to the Ranch that evening to try their luck at catching some Big Browns. I thought it was a great idea so I returned home to await their arrival.

Skip and Gail arrived at the Ranch about 9:30 p.m., ready to go fishing. I suggested we go downriver about a bend and a half, where most of the fish were feeding last night. They agreed.

This stretch of water started with a bend emulating out of a deep chute and a large logjam. It made a large sweeping turn into another bend to the right before passing in front of some cabins. The area was gifted with deep runs and excellent cover for large fish.

I positioned myself at the tail end of the bend. Gail was a little further upstream and Skip was above her. It was now 10:10 p.m. We began to hear several fish beginning to feed. Gail made a couple of casts and took a 17-inch fish. She cast again and took another one, about 16-inches. Skip and I began to wonder if this was ladies' night only.

Finally, a fish fed directly across from Skip. He located it, and allowed it to establish a rhythm and pattern before casting to it. He took the fish from under some tag alders along the bank on his third cast. Skip remarked, "This is a good, heavy fish." We asked if he needed any help. "No," he said, as he battled the trout. The fish made several runs up and down the river trying to tangle Skip's line and break off the fly. The fish didn't know it was at the end of an experienced fisherman's line and had little chance of doing any such thing. Skip finally led the trout over to a sand bar near us and beached it. It was a beautiful, hefty, 21-inch male Brown. I guessed it weighed 4-plus pounds.

While Skip was fighting his battle, I had a fish feed in front of me. My fourth cast hooked it. It was on for about thirty seconds and then it was gone. I had lost it.

As the Spinner fall was nearing its end, another fish fed near Gail, who had moved further upstream. I believe she took this one on her first cast. It was a nice, 18-inch Brown. By the end of the evening Gail had taken three Browns, Skip had caught the largest and I went home empty-handed. Oh well. Regardless of the outcome, I still thoroughly enjoyed the evening because I had spent it with two good friends and two of Grayling's finest fisherpersons, Skip and Gail.

Such is an evening in the life of a Hex fisherman. I knew I wasn't alone in this category, and that I would probably experience other evenings like this; a lot of effort with no results.

Over the years of fishing the Hex hatch, the largest Gail caught was an 8 1/2-pound Brown off the Manistee. Skip's largest was 6-plus pounds. Between the two of them they have caught many, and I mean *many*, Browns between 20 and 24-inches. It was my pleasure to be in such good company.

Since then Skip, Gail and I have fished together on many occasions. We've had some exceptional nights and some not so exceptional. But that's all part of the sport. Irrespective of what happens, I very much enjoy those special moments when we can all fish together.

Whenever I get the opportunity to go to Grayling, my home base is Skip's Sport Shop. If the mood strikes you, stop in and see us.

❊   ❊   ❊

JULY 1997 IS RECORDED AS A MEMORABLE EXPERIENCE, EVEN THOUGH the only involvement I had in the event was that I tied the fly that accomplished this most amazing feat.

Skip and Gail decided to go fishing on the Manistee River one evening. They would anchor the riverboat in a spot where Skip had noticed a large fish feeding the night before, when he was fishing with a friend. This is Gail's story:

> The Spinner fall had just started and the fish Skip had spotted last night was beginning to feed. I saw it feed a couple of times below us. Skip said he wanted to ease the riverboat down another ten feet or so to give me a better angle and a more advantageous casting position. We stopped about twenty-five feet short of where the fish had fed.
>
> I watched a Spinner float down toward the fish and I saw him rise to take it. I immediately cast my fly about five feet above where it fed. I wanted to drop the fly near him because I didn't want him to have much time to look the fly over. (Gail wasn't concerned about spooking the fish because oftentimes Spinners fall at the exact location where fish are feeding and the fish still take them.) The trout took the fly right away, without hesitation. I knew he was big, because when he made the first run he took out all of my fly line — and a significant portion of the backing in a short period of time. I never had a trout do that in all my years of fishing the rivers.
>
> It took thirty-five minutes to land this monster, because it made repeated runs up and down the river, doggedly refusing to come to the net. Every time the fish made a run, Skip maneuvered the riverboat up and down the river to coincide with the run. This gave me the advantage to keep the fish on by keeping my line tight and rod tip high. I

couldn't apply too much pressure as I was fishing with a 5x tippet (which equates to a 4-pound Test).

On one occasion the fish made a run downstream and Skip followed it with the boat as I gathered up the fly line that had come to rest in the bottom of the boat. Then the fish turned and ran upstream. Again we followed it with the boat, but I noticed that the fly line was wrapped around my feet, my pole, the seat, etc. so I frantically untangled the line to let it out. Fortunately, the fish stayed in one location long enough for me to clear the line. If it had made another run it would have broken off because of my tangled fly line. Finally, after a tremendously long battle I brought the fish alongside the boat, belly up (on his side). He was completely exhausted. Skip reached over the side and netted the monster.

Although there were still some flies on the water, the duration of the fight had caused the bigger fish to stop feeding. We called it an evening and went home to measure my catch. The male Brown measured 30 inches and weighed 10 1/4 pounds. What a fish!

What a tremendous accomplishment this was for Gail. Her catch that evening was the largest Brown taken out of the Manistee River in over thirty years.

Gail shared her credit with Skip. She acknowledged that were it not for Skip's excellent maneuvering up and down the river chasing the fish in the riverboat, she would never have landed it.

Skip and Gail received everyone's admiration the next day at their shop. My heartfelt congratulations still goes out to them. It was an exceptional job. I had never seen a Brown this large before, so it was indeed special to share this once-in-a-lifetime feat.

Chapter 4

AU SABLE RIVER FISHING EXPERIENCES

MY DAYS FISHING THE HEX ON THE AU SABLE RIVER ARE MORE numerous than my days fishing on the Manistee. I was initiated to fishing the Hex hatch on the Au Sable over forty years ago, in the late 1950s. From that point forward my enthusiasm has been fed and nurtured by my continual encounters with large Browns.

Over the years my excitement during the Hex hatch has not diminished one iota. In fact, quite the opposite is true. The only difference is that today I am focused on hunting large Browns with the hope of again experiencing a "run for my life" to hook and land one. It is a thrill and a challenge to pit my fishing skills and knowledge against a large Brown's expectations and ability to outwit me within its domain.

In 1958, when I was a young man of twenty, my friends Al Pretto and John Kennedy, and our wives, began the tradition of meeting at Henderson's Lodge (below Wakely Bridge) each June for a precious two weeks of fishing. (We had become good friends when we were students at Michigan State University.) While we fished, our wives occupied their time by visiting Hartwick Pines,

Au Sable River Locations

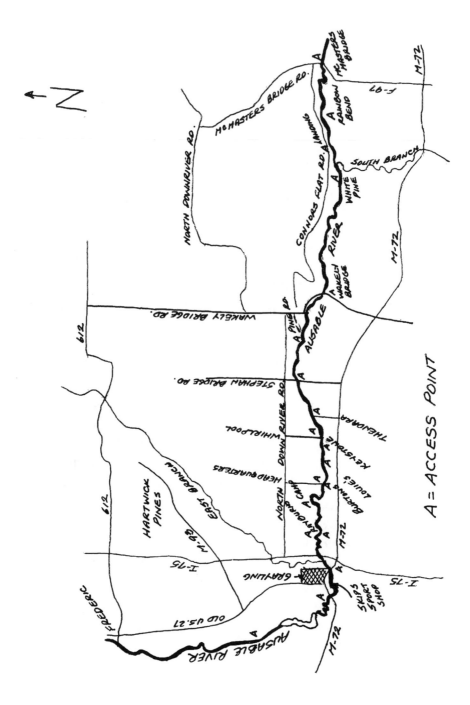

the Fred Bear Museum, Mackinac Island and other favorite attractions. Or sometimes they would spend the entire day on the beach at Lake Margarethe. Once in awhile Al, John and I would spend the day with them, to let them know we still existed. Usually, however, we spent our days fishing, tying flies or scouting out new locations to fish the Hex. And, each day, as the evening drew nearer, we became preoccupied with thoughts of fishing.

On many occasions we would fish a stretch of water known as "Connors Flats" or "Still Water." This was a deep, wide section of water known for its numerous Wiggler beds, long hatches (three, four and five hours in duration) and big fish. Usually we arrived at Connors Flats at 9:00 p.m. We then paddled up to near the mouth of the south branch to fish the Spinner fall and hatch at our select spots. After we felt the hatch was basically over, we would then float back to the landing, constantly casting a vigilant ear toward large feeding fish.

We had developed a system of taking turns to catch trout. As we heard fish feed, Al would try for the first one, then John, then me. The next night John would be first and so forth. This systemized approach typically resulted in four to six large Browns each evening. This was my introduction to fishing the Michigan Hex. I was hooked forever.

Unfortunately, after about ten years of gathering annually, our vocations demanded we be elsewhere; Al in New York, John in Lansing and me in Ohio. This curtailed our ability to get together.

I could write all year long about the many memorable and special moments I shared with Al and John, but these memories could fill a complete book. Maybe, someday, that's what I'll do. I'll always keep these years dear to my heart, as the three of us became inseparable, longtime, fishing buddies.

As schedules permit we get together once in a while to renew our bond by fishing for an evening or two.

🦋   🦋   🦋

I REMEMBER ONE EVENING WHEN THE THREE OF US HAD LEFT Henderson's Lodge to go fishing. We were driving east on M-72 toward McMaster's Bridge road. About halfway into our drive, a big buck sprang out of the ditch, ran parallel with the car for about two hundred feet, and then decided it wanted to get to the other side of the road. In his attempt to hurdle the back end of the car, he caught his hind legs on the deck and made two complete flips in the air before coming to a crash landing on the other side of the road.

We thought that he was surely dead. Al, who was driving the car, immediately hit the brakes and the car came to a stop. As we backed up to see what had happened, I noticed the buck was getting up. He shook himself a couple of times and took off, like a shot out of a cannon, probably wondering what the hell had happened.

What a harrowing experience, especially for me since I was riding in the back seat and was closest to the incident. For a moment I thought I was going to have another passenger join me in the back seat. Wouldn't that have been something? As it turned out, all was well with everyone, including the deer.

Because of this incident we arrived at the river later than usual. As soon as we got there, we paddled extra hard to get to our select spots before they were infiltrated by other fishermen. I was the first one to get out of the canoe, then John went to his spot. Al took the canoe up a little further and parked it. We were about two hundred yards apart from each other on the north side of the river.

It was now about 10:00 p.m., time for the Spinner fall. As expected, the flight bugs began to arrive. For the next ten minutes, the three of us engaged in lively conversation about the status of the flight, whether any fish were feeding and so forth. Suddenly, everything became quiet. We ceased talking. I assumed Al and John had fish starting to feed around them, as I did. I then heard the commotion usually associated with hooking and catching a large fish. It came from the vicinity of both Al and John. I soon learned that they had both taken a nice fish. My creel was empty.

A fish started to feed about fifteen feet in front of me. I took him on my second cast. It was a nice, hefty, 19-inch trout with a jaw slightly beginning to hook upward. The score was even; we each had one.

Then John exclaimed, "I got another one on, and it's nice." From the sound of things I would agree. John landed it after about ten minutes. It was now my turn. As luck would have it, a fish started to feed about thirty feet upriver. Its feeding pattern was extremely unusual as it was bouncing downriver about five feet at a time picking up Spinners. When it got about twenty feet from me, I began casting my fly, each time about five feet shorter. On my sixth cast I finally hooked it, when it was about ten feet away from me. I fought the fish and brought it in. It was a nice, chunky, 18-inch female. The score was now two for John, one for Al and two for me.

John and I then heard some commotion upstream near Al. There was little doubt that he had hooked and was fighting a fish. Al said it was a beauty. After fighting for a bit he finally landed it. The score was even once again.

Three hours passed before Al decided to canoe down and pick up John. The two of them then picked me up. We spent a few minutes surveying our prizes for the evening. Al had a 22-incher and a 20-incher. John's were about 21-inches and 19-inches. I had an 18-incher and 19-incher. The smaller one Al caught was a nice, fat, Rainbow. The others were good, heavy and conditioned Browns.

The night was still young — it was only about 1:00 a.m. - so we decided to cap off our evening by floating back down to the landing, to look for signs of Hatchers and to listen for feeding fish. On our way down we heard a few fish feeding but we couldn't locate them easily. We didn't get out of the canoe until we hit the landing, at about 2:00 a.m. By the time we got organized, put the canoe back on top of the car and drove back to camp, another hour and fifteen minutes had elapsed. It was now 3:15 a.m. and we were exhausted. We said our good-byes for the morning and went to our respective cabins to nestle in our warm beds with our spouses.

This was my first time fishing the Hex Hatch with Al and John. What a night! It was filled with camaraderie, excitement and pure fun. This evening will always rank high on my list of memorable experiences since it was my first successful introduction to fishing the Hex.

Little did I know that our first evening together was only a prelude of the years to come.

🦟   🦟   🦟

I RECALL ANOTHER TIME THAT AL, JOHN AND I FISHED CONNORS FLATS with some success. This particular evening is clear in my mind because of several unusual incidents that occurred.

I had finished tying three dozen Hex flies for our evening's fishing (one dozen for each of us). As I left my cottage, Al and John were just returning from spending the day fishing. (I couldn't go with them because I had to stay home, laboring over the vise, tying flies so we could fish that evening.) They had caught a nice mixture of Brooks, Rainbows and Browns, ranging from 12-inches to 17-inches.

We sat at the picnic table drinking coffee while I listened to Al and John relive catching the trout that were on display in front of me. It was about 8:00 p.m. and we were discussing where we would fish that evening. There was no doubt. Connors Flats won hands down. We agreed to meet at 8:30 p.m. to leave for the Flats.

Eight-thirty rolled around. We loaded our gear into the car and left for the Flats. During the ride I divided up the three dozen flies I had tied. We arrived at our usual landing about 9:10 p.m., unloaded the canoe, put on our gear, loaded our rods, creels, etc. into the canoe and paddled upstream to where we would get out to fish. It was now about 9:50 p.m.

As usual, they dropped me off first. Al got out second and John took the canoe further upstream to his favorite spot. We were positioned about 150 yards apart, which meant that we could see and talk with one another very easily, at least while it was still fairly light. We engaged in some idle conversation while we waited for the Spinner fall to begin. We waited about half an hour before we heard the first fish feed. It was upstream from me and fairly close to Al. I yelled to Al to see if he had heard it. He said he had heard it, and that it was about thirty-five feet away, tight to a logjam. Al made about five or six casts before yelling out that he had lost his fly on a log. He took out one of the flies I had tied for him, and attempted to replace his lost fly. I could see that he had his flashlight on for about ten minutes, apparently trying to tie on a new fly.

During this time there were several fish feeding vigorously around him, and I'm sure Al was beside himself because he hadn't gotten a new fly tied on. Finally he yelled to me, "What the hell is wrong with these flies?"

"I don't know," I replied. "Are you doing it right? Can you see what you're doing? Try to tie on another one."

"I already tried four," he said, "and I can't get any of them tied on."

Trying to conceal my laughter, I said, "Maybe I inadvertently plugged the eyes with cement."

Al, of course, had no idea that I had *purposely* plugged the eyes of his flies. Finally I confessed and told him to take a hook point from one of the flies and punch it through the eyes of the plugged ones, because they were all plugged with head cement.

"I'll get even with you for this," Al promised.

About this time a nice fish began feeding upriver from me about twenty-five feet away, at the end of a large logjam. I worked my way cautiously upstream to a position where I felt I could make the best cast. I cast a couple of times and took nothing. On my third cast I got hooked on a log so I pulled fairly hard and snapped the fly off. I then took my fly box out and grabbed another fly. It was an overcast, dark, evening so, I reached into my upper vest pocket, took out my Mag-Lite and turned it on. Nothing happened. There was no light. I shook it a few times, banged it around, loosened and re-tightened the back end and still no light. I yelled to Al and asked if he had a spare flashlight that I could use. He said he thought so but he wouldn't be down my way for about forty-five minutes. The first nice fish continued to feed as a second one started feeding. I figured out the gist of what Al was doing. He was now paying me back for what I had done to him.

He didn't have to make any extra effort to get even with me as now the shoe was on a different foot, mine. I was being paid back severely for the joke I had pulled on him. What a payback. I had two good fish feeding in front of me with no way to get a fly on my line, or so it seemed. Al began to laugh uncontrollably.

I cleared my mind to collect my thoughts, to see if I could come up with an innovative way to attach my fly to my tippet. After two feeble attempts the conventional way, for some reason, out of pure panic, I tried a completely different approach. The fish were still feeding voraciously and my excitement was growing with each passing minute.

For lack of a better method, I placed the tippet alongside my tongue and began to work the tippet toward the eye of the hook. Amazingly, after two attempts, I slid the tippet through the eye. I then felt my way through, securing the fly with a half-barrel knot. I was now back in business. If you can imagine, this process took the better part of a half-hour and the feeding fish had slowed down, as the prime feeding time was coming to a close.

In a last ditch effort to catch a fish for the evening, I cast my fly for about ten minutes. Much to my chagrin, I took absolutely nothing. I netted a resounding zero for the evening.

I listened intently but heard no other activity. So, I just enjoyed the rest of the evening looking up into the sky, listening to the nocturnal life surrounding the river and wondering what I did wrong to deserve this kind of treatment. I didn't have to look far for the answer. My joke with the plugged flies resulted in a disastrous evening of fishing for me.

After about forty-five minutes of doing nothing, I could hear Al and John making their way down the river, laughing and joking. Al must have told John about my escapades of trying to tie on a fly in total darkness. When they got down to me, I asked how they did. They had each caught two nice fish. Al's were 18 inches and 20 inches. John's were 17 inches and 21 inches. I ended up the goat for the evening with nothing, all because I had tried to inject a little humor into the evening by plugging the eyes of Al's flies.

I knew that Al was gloating because I had received my just dues without him having to put forth any effort. My only reward is that I found a new, innovative way of attaching my tippet to the fly in total darkness. I shared this information with Al and John — but they thought this was poppycock.

When we got back to Henderson's, our base camp, I invited them to my cottage and told them I would try to duplicate the feat I had accomplished at the river. They clothed me with a solid blindfold and said, "Have at it." Lo and behold, out of four attempts, I successfully placed my tippet through the eye of the hook three times, by using my tongue. There were no further jeers or words of disbelief as I had now added credence to my earlier claims.

Since then I have used this method on four separate occasions. It works if you have enough intestinal fortitude and perseverance. Try it yourself. It might come in handy some evening when you experience total darkness.

I learned two very important lessons that evening which will forever be engraved in my mind. First and foremost there is truth in saying "What goes around comes around" and secondly "Where there is a will, there is a way." In any respect, neither one of these prophecies bagged me any fish that evening. I still went home empty-handed — but I was a lot smarter than when I left that evening.

You've probably gathered by now that I've never plugged the eyes on anyone's flies since. In fact, I now make sure that the eye on every fly is clear. Sometimes we have to learn our lessons the hard way, but if we gain valuable knowledge from these unusual experiences, then we are up on the game and can benefit in the future.

※ ※ ※

ONE EVENING AL, JOHN AND I DECIDED TO CHANGE OUR ROUTINE AND try a different fishing spot. Instead of going to Connors Flats we opted for Townline, which was known for its heavy water and big fish. Townline is located approximately three miles by road, down-river from where we were staying at Henderson's Lodge below Wakely Bridge.

We arrived at Townline about 9:15 p.m., unloaded the canoe, packed up our gear and paddled upstream a couple of bends from the landing. These bends contained a multitude of cover in the way of logjams and tag alders, all of which provided an excellent homing ground for large fish.

Our plans were to drop me off at the first bend to the right, and Al and John would proceed further upstream. After we got our act together and made the final preparations to position ourselves at our most strategic locations, it was nearing 10:00 p.m., time for flight bugs to begin.

Al and John had been here several times before, but this was my first time at this location. I familiarized myself with the surround-ings to gauge my fly line distance to two logjams on the opposite bank. Then I sat on a log on shore to wait for the familiar sounds of feeding fish. I could hear Al and John carrying on and laughing upriver, though I could not discern what they were saying.

Finally they stopped talking and yelled down to me that the flies were on the water and some fish were beginning to feed. About that time I heard my first feeding fish near the logjam across the river. I located the fish, made my cautious approach for the best angle to simplify my cast, cast twice and took the fish. It was a 16-inch male Brown, nice and heavy. I listened and it sounded like Al and John had some activity also, but they were too far upriver for me to fully decipher what was going on.

During this time a second fish fed across the river near the jam. I took it on my first cast. It was a 17-inch female in excellent shape. A third fish fed and I took it. Another fed and I took it. I again could hear some rumbling going on upriver, but I didn't pay much attention to what was happening because I was totally involved in the fish feeding in front of me.

The last fish fed, and after several casts and a good fight, I also took it. This was by far the biggest fish of the evening. It was a 19-inch male Brown.

All of this fishing took place within the short span of an hour. I was ecstatic with the evening's undertaking, as I had caught five Browns ranging in size from 16 to 19 inches — truly a bonanza for me.

Since I had my limit and the Spinners had all but ceased coming down the river, I got out of the water and sat on a log awaiting the return of Al and John. About half an hour elapsed before I finally heard activity that indicated they were getting into the canoe to begin their trip downriver to pick me up. It was now about 11:30 p.m. I saw no indication of Hatchers emerging from the mud flats. It appeared that the evening's fishing was over.

Fifteen minutes passed. Finally I saw Al and John round the bend. As they arrived at the shore we exchanged information about how we had done and what flies we had used. Al had caught two trout, an 18-incher and a 16-incher. John had caught one 18-incher. When I emptied my creel, and five nice trout spilled out, I could tell from their response that they were very surprised. "Where in the hell did you catch those?" they asked.

I explained that I had caught them across the river near two log-jams, and that I probably hadn't moved up and down the river more than twenty-five feet to take all of the fish. Apparently I had positioned myself in a honey hole, just loaded with trout. They asked what fly I had been using. "My favorite calf tail Spinner pattern with the brown palmering over the body," I replied.

We got into the canoe and proceeded downriver to the landing. It was customary for us to listen for decent fish that were feeding as we floated downriver. If we heard any we would pull the canoe over and attempt to catch them. We would take turns trying to catch one, depending on how many fish we heard feeding on the way down. Unfortunately, this evening, we didn't hear anything feeding so we got to the landing quickly.

Upon arriving at the landing we perused the water one final time to see if any Hatchers were starting. We didn't see or hear a thing so we decided to call it a night. We de-geared, put everything in the trunk, loaded the canoe and left for home.

Since that evening, there have been a few occasions when I had the pleasure of catching the five trout limit. (Of course, I return to this same location annually to see if I can match my previous feat.) But those evenings don't come along very often in one's lifetime. The evenings that I've been skunked far out number the evenings when I've limited out. Que sera, sera.

I hope that sometime soon you will have the pleasure of catching your limit in one night. I wish you good luck and good fortune in your hunt for Big Browns.

※　※　※

BEFORE BUD DIED, HE AND I HAD THE OPPORTUNITY TO SHARE ANOTHER memorable moment fishing the Hex hatch. It was early in June 1982 when we commenced our second annual Hex fishing expedition.

Realizing that the Hex hatch had not yet started on the Manistee River, Bud and I decided to drive to Skip and Gail's to get the low down on fishing conditions on the Au Sable River. Skip and Gail told us that the hatch had started two or three days earlier and it was beginning to work its way downriver. They said that they were going to fish near Beaver Island that evening with Mel, Lucky and Sam, and that Bud and I were welcome to join them. Bud and I decided to do so. We agreed to meet back at Skip's at 8:00 p.m.

From Beaver Island we would disperse to our favorite fishing grounds. If we spread out we could surround the fish from all directions and maybe one of us would get lucky. I suggested to Bud that he and I drive down to Lucky's property to fish out front, as this had become one of my favorite fishing spots. Not knowing where to go, Bud agreed.

By river, Lucky's was about three bends downriver from Beaver Island. As we approached the river, Skip, Gail, Mel and Sam walked upriver toward Beaver Island while Bud and I drove downriver to Lucky's. When we arrived at our spot we decided to wait half an hour before we put on our fly gear and entered the river, as it was only 8:45 p.m. Half an hour passed. It was now time to prepare for our evening's fishing so, we put on our gear, made our short walk through the woods, entered the river and waded up and across to a bench that was directly across from Lucky's. We were located on a point and could listen both up and downriver.

Bud and I sat on the bench exchanging fishing tales while we waited for the flight bugs to appear against the evening sky. It was a beautiful evening. The warm air (about 65 degrees) provided ideal conditions for a flight and hatch. We were so engrossed in talking that we did not pay much attention to the time. Nor did we set our eyes to the sky to see if there were any Hexes.

It was about 10:20 p.m. — and still no activity. We decided it was time to remain quiet and to listen for feeding fish. After a few more minutes passed I suddenly heard a slurp. It seemed to be upriver, just around the bend from us. I asked Bud if he had heard the noise. He had not. I told him that I was going to get into the river, cross over and wade up a bit to listen.

As I began to wade upstream, I heard a second slurp. Bud heard this one. I waded upriver about fifty feet, stopped and listened for the fish. It fed again and I now had it pinpointed. What a stroke of luck. It was directly across from me about ten feet out from some tag alders on the shore. It was in a good location. No logs, snags or any other trouble.

The fish fed again. I now sized up the situation, stripped off about fifteen feet of line and made my initial cast. Nothing happened. I cast a second and third time — with no results. I knew I was getting a good float because I could see my fly against the moon light on the water's surface. My next cast was about two to three feet further upriver. As it passed over the location where the fish was feeding, I heard a slurp, so I picked up my rod and set the hook. The fish was on, and the fight began.

From the run of line off my reel and the constant power-filled tugging, I could tell that this was a good-sized fish. Bud yelled, "What's going on up there?" Apparently he had heard the fish thrashing around when it came to the surface. I told him I had a real good fish on. Bud said he had one feeding directly in front of him, too. I said for him to have at it and wished him good luck.

About five minutes elapsed, while my fish made several runs and surface rolls as it tried to free itself. Sam, who was upriver about two hundred yards, also heard the commotion and yelled "What the hell are you doing down there, making all that noise?" I yelled back that it wasn't me but the fish I had on and was about to land. Sam continued to ask me questions about whether or not I had landed it, how big it was, etc. I responded that I didn't know yet and didn't have time to talk, as I needed to concentrate on getting my fish in.

I worked the fish back upriver and brought it near me. As it was thrashing vigorously in front of me, I netted it. It was a nice, conditioned, hefty male that I guessed to be 21 or 22 inches.

I went back down to where Bud was. He had bagged a 17 1/2-incher. We decided to sit for awhile and listen for other fish. While waiting, we measured my fish. It was 22 inches on the money. What a nice start to the evening. We were both ready for the second round.

As we were sitting, we heard a fish feeding upriver. I asked Bud if he'd like to give it a shot, but he said no.

Off I went again. This fish was near a logjam. As I was making my way up, another fish fed behind me. Bud heard it and said that he would try his hand at this one. I continued wading until I got directly across from the logjam. There I stood, waiting, when I heard the fish feed again. It was tight to a log at the end of the jam; a tough spot, but nothing ventured, nothing gained. I stripped off about twenty-five feet of line and cast my fly about ten feet above the fish. Fortunately, I got a beautiful first float and the fish took it. I could tell that this fish wasn't as big as my first one, but it was decent. As I was fighting my fish, I heard familiar fighting noises downstream, so I called to Bud. He said that he had a good one on. I asked if he needed help. He said he didn't know. I quickly landed mine, about a 17-inch female, and proceeded down to help Bud.

As I got there, Bud was still fighting the fish, but it had gone to the bottom and was sulking, as they often do. I suggested that he thump the bottom of his rod with his palm to cause vibration in the line. He did and the fish took off for another run. Bud worked it over to me and I netted it for him. It was a nice fish. We then got out of the water and retired back to our bench. Bud's fish measured 18 1/2 inches.

It was now about 11:30 p.m. and the activity had slowed down. We waited for another fifteen minutes and then decided to leave. We were both happy with the evening's productivity, even though we didn't do great harm to the fish population. We each had two nice fish, and decided that this was enough. We waded back across the river, made our way through the trees and back to the car. As preplanned, we would now go to the Big Boy's in town for coffee and a little something to eat. We arrived first, then the rest of the group appeared one by one until all seven of us were there.

Skip, Gail, Mel, Lucky and Sam collectively caught about five fish ranging in size from 14 to 18 inches. Prior to eating, the first order of business was to look at my 22-incher since it was the biggest catch of the evening. Everyone extended his or her congratulations as we went back into the restaurant. After eating and discussing the evening's fishing experiences, we departed for our respective domiciles, as it was now about 1:30 a.m.

Bud and I enjoyed several other productive evenings fishing the Hex hatch that year, but that was the biggest fish caught that season.

I'm very glad Bud and I had the opportunity to fish that year, as it was the last time we would be together. I hope that wherever he is, Bud is enjoying the peace, tranquility and friendship that we always shared while fishing the Hex on the Manistee and Au Sable rivers. God bless my buddy! Maybe some day in the future we will be able to reunite and once again share our love of trout fishing.

※　※　※

THE LAST TWO WEEKS IN JUNE 1991 FOUND ME ENDING THE HEX HATCH with one of my most productive years when it came to large fish. That season I enjoyed the good fortune of catching five fish between 18 and 22 inches (one 18-incher, one 19-incher, one 20-incher, one 20 1/2-incher and one 22-incher). These fish were taken within a span of four days at the same location, some twelve miles east of town on Route 72, several bends below Wakely Bridge. It was a year that I could do no wrong. I hooked and landed every fish I cast my fly to — a rare feat.

My most memorable experience occurred near the end of the hatch with my long-time fishing buddy, Mike Caswell. We elected to fish this location because it was one of the last places to get flies and because it produced fish in the 21 to 24-inch class year after year. We didn't expect anything different this year.

We had fished the spot three nights in a row, and together we had taken six trout in the 18 to 20 1/2-inch range. This particular evening Mike and I left town early, drove the twelve miles to our spot and arrived about 9:00 p.m., an hour before we would expect the Hex flight bugs to appear. Word had gotten out that Mike and I had done fairly well the previous three evenings, so we had to get there early to solidify our favorite spots for the evening.

We suited up and entered the river. Mike, as usual, elected to wade downriver to a spot where he had hooked several good fish the previous year. I decided to camp out at the landing to fish a wide, deep, sweeping bend, which always held good fish. It was now about 9:15 p.m.

Mike and I engaged in several conversations, discussing the weather, whether or not the bugs would come and last year's fishing experiences at this location. While we were talking more and more fishermen appeared. Many positioned themselves between Mike and me, and some settled upriver from me. Time passed quickly. It was nearing 10:00 p.m. so we agreed to settle down and prepare for the arrival of the flight bugs.

We began to detect a few flight bugs flying upstream so we made the necessary preparations to commence fishing. We ceased all conversation and began listening for the usual feeding sounds associated with flies on the water. We heard some smaller fish feed but everyone waited patiently, listening for sounds of a big fish.

It was now about 10:50 p.m. and the Spinners began to slow down. The activity on the water's surface grew less and less. It appeared to be one of those fruitless nights when no decent fish would feed. Because of the inactivity most of the fishermen began to leave. In fact, ten minutes later it was just Mike and me left to hunt for large trout. A few Spinners were still floating on the surface but we didn't hear any activity around us.

Finally Mike said he had one on and it felt like a really good fish. I asked if he needed some help "By the time you get down here it will probably be too late," he exclaimed I could hear Mike's fish thrashing around when it came to the surface. Mike called out again to reaffirm that it was a good-sized fish. He said that it was taking line and had about fifty feet out when suddenly there was silence. I could hear Mike utter several words of dismay, so I asked what happened. He said that during the last run the fish had broken off. We were both upset at the termination of his fight, as it had been a long evening with nothing to show for our efforts. Mike said he was coming back upriver to join me.

As he waded upriver towards me I heard a fish feed about fifteen feet away, directly in front of me, but I didn't fish for it for fear of putting a larger fish down. Mike finally got back up to the landing and we discussed the circumstances surrounding the fish he had just lost. By this time it was about 11:30 p.m. and there was no activity on the water at all. We decided we would stay until 12:15 a.m., to see if any Hatchers would emerge from the muck beds.

At about 11:45 p.m. we took out our flashlights and surveyed the water for signs of Hatchers. Much to our surprise, several

Hatchers began floating down the river, so we got more serious about our plan. We waited, but nothing happened.

At exactly midnight we heard what sounded like two or three fish feeding across river, near a logjam in an eddy with a reverse current. After a few minutes we pinpointed their location.

We made our way slowly into the river to a place about fifteen to twenty feet away from where they were feeding. Mike gave me the honor of trying to catch one of them. Realizing that I still had a Spinner pattern on, I told Mike it might be beneficial if we tied on a Hatcher, which is what we did. I then positioned myself so that I could present the fly as naturally as possible. This was an extremely difficult area to fish because the water was deep, there were several snags to get hung up on, the current we had to fish over was swift and there was a reverse current in the eddy where the fish were feeding. All of these issues had to be considered because each posed a hurdle to be overcome.

As Mike watched, I cast my fly from every possible position for forty-five minutes. Even though the fish continued to feed voraciously, not one fish came and looked at my fly, let alone bite! For the life of me I couldn't figure out what was wrong. After expending my energy, I turned to Mike and said, "Have at it, it's your turn."

For the next forty-five minutes Mike cast his fly from every possible angle — and met with the same results. Not one strike between us after one-and-a-half hours of fishing. We felt somewhat intimidated and outsmarted by the fish that we were hunting.

By this time the hatch was coming to an end. We decided to call it quits for the evening. During our trip home we discussed in detail what had taken place. Neither of us could come up with an answer. All we knew was there were several decent fish feeding on Hatchers and we didn't take one of them. What a frustrating evening it had been.

The only positive thing to come out of it was the challenge that had been set for our next night's fishing. There was no doubt about where we were going to fish. We agreed to meet again the following evening to try for a second time to take one of the 20-plus-inch fish that we assumed were there.

At 8:30 p.m. Mike and I again drove to the same location twelve miles east of town. When we arrived at the river, there were already several cars parked there. Word had spread that the Hexes were still on at this location. Luckily, there was no one at our landing. Mike and I were the only people who knew about the fish feeding across the river in the eddy — and we were not about to tell anyone.

Our plan was to skip the Spinner fall, if it came, for fear of spooking the large fish that we had located. We were going to wait it out until the Hatchers started.

At about 9:30 p.m. we suited up and waded out a short distance into the river. This was quite early for the Hatchers but we didn't want anyone to take our spot for the evening. If you snooze, you lose — so it's important to pick your place early.

As it approached 10:00 p.m. quite a few fishermen positioned themselves in the river, both upstream and downstream from us, in anticipation of the Spinner fall.

About half an hour went by before we heard fish feeding on the Spinners as they fell to the water. Mike and I heard several decent fish feeding — but we refrained from fishing — which was extremely hard to do. Our consolation was that none of the fish sounded as large as the fish we heard feeding on the Hatchers the previous night.

Another half-hour went by. We heard several fish taken by the fishermen around us. The trout were nice, in the 14 to 16-inch category, but nowhere near the size of the fish we were stalking.

At about 11:15 p.m. the peak of the activity stopped and all of the other fishermen left. It was only Mike and me. This is what we wanted, the two of us to await the hatch. Apparently the other fishermen were fairly new at this game and didn't know about the possibility of Hatchers coming out later in the evening or early in the morning.

Mike and I engaged in idle conversation while we waited for the Hatchers to start. As the night before, at exactly midnight the same fish began feeding in the eddy across from the landing. In fact, the timing was so precise you could have set your watch by it.

Mike and I had agreed that we would follow the same format as the previous night. Once again I positioned myself in the same location as the night before and commenced to fish.

I cast and cast and cast my fly, from every angle possible, for the next forty-five minutes — without a strike. I turned to Mike and said, "I don't know what's wrong but I can't get anything to take my fly, no matter what I do. It's your turn to try."

Mike took over and cast his fly for about twenty minutes — without any luck. He decided to cross the river and approach them from a different angle. I was to act as his spotter and let him know where his fly was in relationship to the feeding fish. As Mike continued to cast his fly I spotted for him, but all was in vain, because he didn't have any luck either.

We couldn't figure out what was happening. We didn't think we were doing anything wrong. This was a very unusual situation for two fishermen with sixty-five years of experience fishing the Hex hatch between them. (It just goes to show that when you think you have it all figured out, another glitch appears.)

After about another ten minutes the fish all but ceased to feed, as the Hatchers had slowed down. Can you imagine, over three hours of hard fishing the past two nights and not even a strike? What a bummer!

Mike came back across the river. We got out, went to the car, unsuited and left for home, completely baffled. On the way home we discussed in detail what the problem might be and why we couldn't take any fish.

Suddenly I had a flashback from years earlier, when I had been in a similar situation. Maybe, just maybe, this wasn't two or three fish feeding but only one fish that was cruising along the mud banks picking up all the Hatchers it could. If this were the case then the fish wouldn't establish any feeding pattern. It would just cruise along from spot to spot picking up Hatchers at random. At least this was a new theory that would give us something different to look forward to later this evening. We would use a completely different approach to take this fish — along with lots of perseverance and patience.

When we returned to Mike's car he said he had some work he must do and that he would not be able to fish for a couple of days. This meant I wouldn't have a partner that night. It would be up to my skills and me.

There was no question as to where I would fish later that evening, as the challenge grew more and more complex. I would continue with the same pattern set the previous two nights, only this time I would have an alternate plan. My curiosity was aroused as to what was going on in the eddy.

About 8:00 p.m. that evening I left for the same fishing spot with a totally revised plan of attack. I would treat "these fish" as a solo cruiser and adjust my thoughts accordingly. I arrived at my destination about 8:30 p.m., suited up for the evening and took my place in the river, waiting for the midnight feeding. This was extremely early to be getting into the river, but again, I didn't want anyone to take my spot. Ten p.m. rolled around and I could see some flight bugs beginning to make their way upriver.

About 10:30 p.m. I began to hear a few fish starting to feed on Spinners. I heard a decent fish feed a little downstream from where I was, so I moved down about twenty feet and heard it feed some fifteen feet in front of me under an overhanging branch. I decided

61

that since it was early enough, I might as well try for it. At least I wouldn't go home empty-handed for a third night in a row. I took the fish on my second cast. It was a nice, hefty, 17-inch female Brown. She gave me an excellent fight in the strong current before I netted her. I then decided to stop fishing the Spinner fall. At least I had one trout in my hand, which was a lot better than the previous nights when I received the "El Skunko" award.

I regrouped, tied on a Hatcher and anxiously waited for the Hatchers to start. If everything was the same, the hatch would start at about 11:45 p.m. which was an hour and fifteen minutes away. As it grew nearer to the bewitching hour, I got more and more excited in anticipation of catching a large Brown.

At about 11:55 p.m. the landing began to get cluttered with all kinds of activity from fishermen coming in and riverboats docking. I chatted with some people at the landing for about five minutes and told them I was waiting for a particular fish to start feeding on the Hatchers. Just as I finished my conversation, again, exactly at midnight, one or more fish began to feed in the eddy.

I shined my light toward the mud flats above and saw that the Hatchers were emerging out of the muck. I remained somewhat calm and tried to identify what was occurring. Suddenly, I noticed a fish take a Hatcher across from me, a few seconds later another one, then a Hatcher ten feet upstream, and a few seconds later, another Hatcher was about five feet below.

Since I had changed my approach from thinking that this was two or three fish feeding to one cruiser picking up Hatchers at random, I watched and listened for about five minutes to see if I could make some sense out of the feeding cycle. I decided that when the fish fed across from me, I would count to ten and throw my fly ten feet further above, near the second location. I cast my fly several times but nothing happened.

The fish fed in front of me again. I false cast a couple of times and cast my fly about five feet further upriver than before. About four feet into the float I heard the familiar slurp, so I picked up my rod and set the hook. "I got it!" I yelled. "And it's a good one."

The fish came to the surface, made a large splash and ran downriver about fifty feet. All of the people at the landing, some twenty-five feet below me, began to cheer me on and chant words of encouragement.

The fish turned and ran upriver about seventy feet. It felt extremely strong, particularly in the deep water and fast current. I applied pressure and it turned again, ran downriver for about forty feet, stopped and went to the bottom, shaking its head from side to side trying to ditch my fly. I thumped the bottom of my rod. It surfaced, rolled around and came toward me. It was now about twenty feet in front of me, where it made several sideward movements and short runs. All this time the people at the landing were constantly talking to me and asking, "Is it still on? Is it a good one? Where is it?" One voice yelled out, "Bring it toward me and I'll net it for you." I said I would do just that.

I slowly worked the fish over to the landing and this gentleman, who I later found out was the sheriff, placed his net in the water, hit the fish in the nose and the fish took off again. This occurred three different times (luckily he didn't knock the fly out). Finally I said, in a nice way, that I thought it would be easier if I just beached the fish at the landing.

I again worked the fish to the landing, walked up on shore and beached the fish about five feet on shore. I didn't want to make the sheriff feel bad but I also didn't want to lose the fish I had worked so hard for over the last three evenings. I thanked the sheriff for his efforts and was as diplomatic as I could be, for reasons I need not explain.

Once I got the fish on shore the fly popped out of its mouth. It was a good thing this didn't happen when the sheriff banged him on the nose with his net three different times. Everyone gathered around while we measured the fish. It was a hook-jawed, male

Brown that measured a little over 22 inches and weighed approximately 3 1/2 pounds. What a nice catch! I was happy, even though it had taken three nights of hard fishing before I figured out it was one fish rather than two or three.

You may be able to use this sort of information in your hunt for Big Browns. Just remember, cruisers are the most difficult to catch because they don't establish any particular feeding pattern and you don't have any inkling of where they are going to pick up their next fly. Sometimes you just have to wait them out and maybe they will make a mistake or you'll get lucky, like I did. All in all I was pleased with the evening since I had a 17-inch and a 22-inch fish in my possession.

I waited around for another fifteen minutes to see if I could hear any other fish feeding in the eddy. I didn't, so I guess my cruiser theory proved to be right.

I broke down my rod, walked up to the car, put everything in the trunk and left for home. Fortunately, I would now have a story for Mike when he returned.

On one other occasion I was confronted with a similar situation, but I never took the fish, even after four nights of fishing. I conceded defeat.

Such is trout fishing during the Hex hatch. You either score or you don't. These unsuccessful events do not minimize the anticipation, excitement and pure enjoyment each time you hit the river in search of trophy Browns. They just enhance your burning desire.

After I returned to the motel I froze the fish and later took him home to have him mounted.

✸   ✸   ✸

AFTER I SOLD THE TROUT RANCH MY DAUGHTER, KATE, AND I ENJOYED two evenings fishing the Michigan May fly hatch together. The first time occurred in the late eighties. Kate called me near the end of my vacation. She wanted to come north to Grayling to spend two or three days with me before I returned home. I telephoned her mother and made arrangements to pick Kate up in St. Johns, which is located some seventeen miles north of Lansing. On Thursday of that week I drove down to St. Johns, picked up my daughter and returned to Grayling.

When we arrived in Grayling, we drove by the trout ranch, visited some friends we knew and then went to Skip and Gail's Sport Shop, where we stayed until about 5:00 p.m. We then went to our favorite restaurant, the Lone Pine, for dinner and visited with John and Marilyn (the owners) for awhile. We left the restaurant about 7:00 p.m. to return to the motel for some R & R before embarking on our fishing trip. I decided that we would fish at a location about twelve miles east of town. This spot was usually one of the last places on the main stream to receive large Hexes, and it typically held big fish.

We left the motel about 9:00 p.m. (which is somewhat later than usual). I didn't think there would be much competition on the river considering it was Thursday and the hatch was abruptly nearing its end for the year. We arrived at the river about 9:40 p.m. We soon realized that fate had dealt us a pat hand as there was absolutely no one else in sight. We had this section of river to ourselves.

We got out of the car and walked around for a few minutes to take a look at the river, enjoying its serenity and tranquillity, before I suited up to prepare for an evening of fishing. Kate decided to get back into the car before the nightly onslaught of mosquitoes began. They didn't let us down. I told Kate that I was going to wait in the river for about half an hour to see if any flies appeared. If nothing happened I would call it quits for the evening. It was about 10:00

p.m. and if there were going to be any flies they would start soon. Another fifteen minutes went by without any activity. Ten more minutes passed and still no action.

Just as I was about to exit the river I heard what I considered to be a decent fish feed around the bend and upriver about fifty feet. I cautiously waded upriver so I could better locate the fish. I listened. It fed again, to the right about twenty feet directly in front of me. I thought about repositioning myself so that I wouldn't have to cast the fly and line over the top of the fish, but rationale got the better part of me. I knew that fish became very selective and extremely spooky about any movement in the water this late in the hatch. So I said to myself, "What the hell. This will probably be the last fish I'll try to catch during this year's hatch, " and I gently cast my fly over the fish in hope of enticing a strike. The fish fed again, but in a different location. I listened closely. It fed another time, but again in a different location. I now surmised that it was cruising along, picking up all of the Spinners it could, trying to get one final meal of May flies before the season ended.

I stripped out some line and began to gently cast my fly over the fish in several directions, always quietly picking up my fly and gently casting it again. I cast my fly ten or twelve times before I finally heard a slurp in the general direction of where I had gauged my fly to be. As I picked up my rod tip, I felt the power I had been anticipating all evening. The fish was on. It made a strong run upstream for about fifty feet. I turned it and it ran across river to some logs, probably in an effort to tangle me up to gain its freedom. I turned it again, at which time it ran downstream for about forty or fifty feet. The fish felt extremely strong in the fast current of the river. I had no inclination of how big it was at this point, I only knew that it was a good fish and my mind was dedicated to getting it in. As the fish ran downstream, I waded downstream, constantly gathering in the slack line so I wouldn't lose the tension on the fish. One thing I knew for certain was that I definitely could

not wade downriver as quickly as the fish swam downstream. It was a precarious position to be in, especially when I had to be concerned about the current and wading over and around obstacles, such as logs and other debris.

The fish came to rest about ten feet below the landing. My biggest hurdle was to get the fish in without losing it. I worked it around by retrieving more line so that it was exactly in front of the landing. I began walking backward up the landing, always keeping tension on the line, until I beached the fish on the ground portion of the landing. It was aimlessly flopping around, trying to get back into the water. I dropped my rod, walked the line down and grabbed my prize. It was a hefty 19 1/2-inch female Brown. She had the biggest girth of any fish I'd ever caught. She was shaped like a football. I guessed her to weigh 3 1/2-plus pounds.

I picked up my rod and the fish and returned to the car to show Kate my catch for the evening. She was fast asleep on the front seat of the car, without a care in the world. I banged on the window, woke her up and showed her my fish. She was very happy for me. After placing my gear in the trunk, we left for the motel. On our way back we were fortunate to see four lovely deer in their natural environment. This was one of the gifts nature provided us, with no remuneration. We returned to the motel about midnight, talked for a bit and then went to sleep.

The following two days, Friday and Saturday, Kate and I spent visiting friends, relaxing and sightseeing. I didn't fish at all. Saturday evening we packed our bags in preparation for our departure on Sunday morning. My season's fishing was capped off by catching this last large Brown, which actually turned out to be my second largest fish for the year. It was a heartfelt pleasure to have my daughter with me to share this experience.

❋

The next year Kate again spent the last three days of my vaca-

tion with me in Grayling. Only this time we spent the last night fishing one of the tributaries of the main stream. Kate actually waded the river with me, as the current was slower and the water less deep than the main stream. Kate must be my good luck charm, as once again I was fortunate to catch two nice Browns (one 18-inches and one 19-inches) to cap off the season's fishing.

✺

As Kate grew older her interests became more diversified. We parted ways for awhile and stopped meeting during my annual three-week fishing vacation in Grayling. This saddened me, but I had the memories of those two very special years when Kate and I spent quality time together by sharing in the sport that she knew I loved so dearly. Several years lapsed before we would meet in Grayling again.

Our most recent reunion in Grayling occurred in June 1998 when Kate and her boyfriend, Joshua, came to visit me for four days. This reunion rekindled my feelings and brought back memories of old. Even though Kate is now twenty-one, I still have very special thoughts of when she and I shared our life and love together for a few precious days. I will cherish them forever. I look forward to the time when Kate and I can once again share our life and love together, regardless of the occasion.

Kate, I will always love you very, very much. Thanks for being so understanding when I fished while you were with me in Grayling. And, my dear, please stay in touch, for time grows shorter each day.

My eternal love, Dad

✺   ✺   ✺

IN THE LATE 1980S, A CHAIN OF EVENTS INVOLVING AN INDIVIDUAL WHO shall remain anonymous occurred. This person is a very good friend of mine. We worked together at the Chrysler Jefferson plant for many years.

As I recall, I was about ready to depart for my annual two-week vacation in Grayling, to tie flies and to fish for Big Browns. Mr. X, as he shall be known from this point on, began to display a sincere interest in fly-fishing and said he would like to try fishing for Browns on the Au Sable River during the Hex Hatch.

We made the necessary arrangements. He was to join me in Grayling the following weekend. Earlier that week my daughter, Kate, would join me for a few days of relaxation.

As Thursday rolled around, Jim (oops, I mean Mr. X) appeared at Skip's Sport Shop. He was excited about the next several evenings of fishing we were about to embark on. I made all of the formal introductions at the shop, after which Mr. X proceeded to purchase waders, leaders, flies, tippets, and all the other sundries needed to fish for Browns at night during the Hex Hatch.

I realized that Mr. X was getting very excited about the possibility of catching a Big Brown, especially after listening to Skip, Gail and me relive some of our fishing experiences.

After organizing his equipment, we took the rod, which Skip had loaned to Mr. X, behind the shop so that I could impart my knowledge of fly-fishing to Mr. X. I explained the basic fundamentals of fly-fishing regarding grip, casting the fly, mending the line, etc., for about an hour and a half. At that point I felt comfortable with Mr. X's performance.

He appeared to progress well in such a short period of time and was casting the fly fairly decently. Upon our completion of the training session, Mr. X, Kate, and I left the shop to eat dinner at the Lone Pine restaurant. After finishing our dinner, we proceeded back to our motel rooms for some rest before going fishing. We agreed to meet outside of the Woodland Motel about 8:30 p.m.

At 8:30 we met in front of our rooms, packed the gear into the car and left for the river. I selected a location called Townline. It was late in the season and I felt there would be some flight bugs and hatchers at this spot.

We arrived at the river about 9:15 p.m. Mr. X and I suited up and got into the river, as Kate watched. I wanted Mr. X to get the feel of casting the fly and seeing it float downriver before nighttime befell us and we began some serious fly-fishing. He appeared to be comfortable and was casting the fly well enough to actually catch a fish.

As 10:00 p.m. approached I began to explain to Mr. X that we should be looking into the sky to see if we could see any flight bugs. This we did, and I began to point out some Hexes to Mr. X. After a couple of minutes of watching the sky and me continuously identifying Hexes that were flying upstream, Mr. X saw a few on his own. He grew more excited.

The night was very dark and cloudy, with only a sliver of a moon offering us any light. After a short while we heard a fish feed. We listened, while I identified the sounds that indicated a feeding fish. Mr. X began to hear a few fish, but he couldn't locate them. I began to tell Mr. X where the fish were and how to approach them.

As his fly floated over a fish I saw it take the fly. I exclaimed to Mr. X., "Pick up your rod tip." He did, but it was too late. The fish escaped his hook. This happened several times. Mr. X couldn't get the hang of hooking fish.

After a few casts, Mr. X said that his rod tip felt funny. I told him the line was probably wrapped around the tip. Upon checking his rod, I discovered that this was indeed the problem. This happened several times, and each time I would unscramble the line for him. At one point the line was so snarled at the tip that it looked like a bird's nest.

After several attempts at catching fish and several line wrappings, Mr. X became discouraged — and gave up. He left the river and returned to the car, where Kate was waiting.

I stayed in the river, until they honked the car horn a couple of times, asking for me to return to the car. I had managed to catch a couple fish.

This was both the start and the demise of Mr. X's fly-fishing experience. I vividly remember that the only utterance I heard was "How in the hell can you see what you're doing? It's so dark, I can't even see my hand in front of my face, let alone the fly on the water."

Mr. X never attempted to fly-fish again. In fact, he gave me his waders, net, and the other sundries the very next day. Since then, Mr. X has become a different sort of fisherman. He fishes with a guide on several lakes in Florida, for Bass — in the daylight. Apparently fly-fishing was not his cup of tea.

Mr. X, if you read this, and would like to try the Hex Hatch again, just say the word. I would give it another shot.

Your dear friend, Dan

❋   ❋   ❋

My dear friend Eric Swander and I have fished together on many occasions. I remember one evening in particular though, when both of us were fortunate enough to bag several nice fish.

It was near the end of the hatch. Eric and I met at Skip's about 8:30 p.m. From Skip's we drove about twelve miles out of town to one of our favorite spots, where we knew the Hex hatch historically lasted longer.

We arrived at our destination about 9:15 p.m. We knew the hatch was in its final days as there were no other fishermen around. Eric and I suited up. We positioned ourselves in the river at our usual spots and waited for the flight bugs to begin making their way upriver. It was about 9:50 p.m.

We talked for about ten minutes, then decided to remain quiet so that we could look and listen for any signs of a hatch. After about ten minutes, we heard our first evidence of fish beginning to feed. In fact, we heard one decent fish upstream. Eric decided to go after it. As he was wading upstream, I heard a fish feed directly across river and a little upstream from where I was standing. We both waited until each fish fed a couple more times before attempting to catch them.

After several casts, Eric finally yelled out, "I got one and it feels fairly good". I asked if he needed any help. "No," he said, "not right now." He no sooner got the words out of his mouth and I hooked the one I was fishing for. If Eric needed my help now, he was out of luck, since I was preoccupied with my fish. We fought the fish for a few minutes before landing them. Eric's was a nice 163/4-inch male Brown. Mine was an 18-inch male. We congratulated each other and listened again for other feeding fish.

The hatch continued for another half-hour. As the evening came to a close, Eric and I had bagged five fish, three for Eric and two for me. Eric's were 16 3/4 inches, 15 inches and 14 inches. Mine were 20 inches and 18 inches. It was an excellent evening of fly-fishing.

Eric and I fish together at least once a year during the Hex hatch. It is always a pleasure to share time with him, even though he is about thirty-four years younger than I am. The bonds of friendship and fly-fishing don't discriminate against age. I'm sure Eric and I will continue to share special moments together, as we both look forward to the Hex hatch each year. Nothing will sever the bond that we have developed and I know that I am a richer person for it.

Best of everything to you always, Eric.

Your friend, Dan

꙰ ꙰ ꙰

JOHN SCHNEIDER, ANOTHER YOUNGSTER OF THIRTY-THREE OR THIRTY-four, and I have become good friends and fishing companions over the years. John is a Grayling resident and a distributor of fishing equipment. I met John in Skip's Sport Shop about ten years ago when I was tying flies for the Hex hatch, which was in the full speed mode on the Manistee and Au Sable rivers. John displayed an interest in learning how to tie the flies, so I began giving him pointers each time he came into the shop. He was a quick learner and readily picked up all of the information I was willing to divulge, even about my secret Hex fly patterns.

John has since become an excellent fly-tier — almost as good as his mentor — if that's possible. (Only joking.) We have fished together on several occasions, but one special evening sticks in my mind more clearly than others. It occurred in the early nineties at my favorite location twelve miles out of town on the main stream of the Au Sable.

John and I left Skip's together and arrived at our location about 9:30 p.m., which was late if we expected to get a good position in the river. Fortunately for us, there were hardly any fishermen and we had the pick of the river in front of and down from the landing. We hurriedly got into our gear and positioned ourselves in the river, anxiously awaiting first the Spinners and then the Hatchers. After several minutes, a few fish began feeding, but nothing worthwhile. We waited a few more minutes and heard nothing, so John decided to wade downriver a bit. I remained in my usual location.

Finally, John yelled out that he had a decent fish on and he might need some help. I told him that my help was there for the asking, but he should hurry because I heard a good fish that had started to feed. John landed his fish, which measured 18 1/2 inches in length. It was a nice Brown.

The fish I was after was feeding steadily, so I decided to give it my college all. After about the third cast the fish took my fly. It felt real good. I guessed it was in the 20-plus-inch class. After several strong forceful runs the fish began to come toward me. I placed my net in the water twice but it doggedly refused to come to the net. I decided to beach it on the landing. It was a nice 20-inch male Brown, in excellent condition.

While I was fighting my fish, John had hooked and landed another Brown, which he guessed to be about 16 1/2 to 17 inches.

It was now about 11:30 p.m. John and I decided to wait until midnight to see if any Hatchers would oblige us by coming out, but it cooled down too quickly and none appeared. We decided to call it an evening. Not a bad night's fishing, with John bagging an 18 1/2-incher and a 17-incher, and me taking a 20-incher.

It is especially enjoyable for me to fish with younger people like John and Eric. It allows me the opportunity to share my fly-fishing knowledge and experiences and to continue the legacy of pursuing and capturing Big Browns during the Hex hatch.

It was my good fortune to share this evening of serenity, camaraderie and friendship with my good friend John. I'm sure that if the Lord is willing John and I will share more special events in years to come. John, keep practicing your fly tying! I don't know if there are enough years to become as good as me — but at least you'll be second.

Your friend, Dan

❋   ❋   ❋

TEN FORTY-FIVE P.M. ON THURSDAY, JUNE 24, 1993 IS ETCHED IN MY mind as my most memorable experience fishing the Hex hatch on the Au Sable River in Grayling, Michigan.

Earlier that evening Lucky Luckstead, Mike Caswell and I were engaged in our usual conversation at Skip's, trying to decide where we would fish that night. Knowing that the Hex hatch had just started we unanimously agreed to fish in front of Lucky's place, since the hatch typically occurred there first. We decided to meet at Lucky's about 9:15 p.m. and from there we would go our separate ways, as had always been the case in the past.

As usual, upon meeting, we donned our usual paraphernalia and dispersed to our favorite spots. Lucky and Mike went downriver to where Mud Creek dumps into the Au Sable. This stretch of water supported numerous Wiggler beds (muck) and presented an excellent location for feeding fish. I chose to stay in front of Lucky's property, as I do every year since this spot has afforded me the good fortune of catching several large Browns (one 19-inches, one 20-inches and one 22-inches) over the past several years. My hope was to repeat my past performances, if fate would see it so fitting.

I waded across the river and up against the current about one hundred feet. I would sit on a bench on the shore directly across from Lucky's, in quiet anticipation of the long-awaited Hex flight and hatch.

At about 9:45 p.m. I looked into the sky to see if I could detect any flight bugs making their way upriver. There was nothing yet, so I decided to enjoy nature's offerings.

The moon began to lift higher in the sky and cast a brilliant light on the Au Sable. What a sight to behold! The moon's reflection on the water, surrounded by mirrored images of the pines and cedars, created a scene that is usually captured on canvas. Several nocturnal animals began to express their nightly calls, creating a symphony in the night. I noticed the woodcocks and nighthawks going through their evening flights, casting dark shadows against the moonlit sky. Such beauty and grace nature bestows on us, which, unfortunately, is so often taken for granted.

I became so engrossed in Mother Nature's beauty and serenity that I *almost* forgot why I was there to - to entice a Big Brown to take my Hex pattern and let the fight begin.

It was now about 10:00 p.m. Again I looked into the sky to see if I could detect any indications of a May fly flight. After about five minutes I saw a few Hexes making their way upstream to mate. I now gathered my senses and prepared my rod and reel for battle.

Ten minutes went by with no activity. Another five minutes passed with no activity. Then, I finally heard the familiar slurp that I'd been anxiously awaiting. I poised my ears toward the direction of the slurp to decipher its location. After a couple more slurps I had pinpointed the fish under a cedar overhanging the river.

I stripped out about fifteen feet of line and cast it above where the fish was feeding. As my line passed over the area where the fish fed, I heard a slurp. I picked up my rod tip and felt a tug. Fish on. No. Fish off. It struck but I didn't set the hook solidly. Maybe I had too much slack in the line. Well, that's number one I put down for the evening. The score was: fish, one; Dan, zero. Let's try for number two.

I waited a few minutes and heard another fish feed some twenty yards downriver from where I was standing. I gingerly made my way downriver to an advantageous position and listened. I waited a few more minutes and the fish fed again. I now had it located some two feet off the shore, near some tag alders.

I stripped off about ten feet of line and cast upstream about six feet. As the line floated over the exact location, the fish fed. I again picked up the rod tip and felt a tug. Fish on. No. Fish off. Damn, missed another one that probably will not feed again this evening.

I've been in this predicament before, when I've nicked three or four fish in an evening only to go home empty-handed. Thoughts began running through my mind. Was it the moon? Was it the leader? Was it the fly? Was the line too slack? Or was my timing off, seeing that I hadn't done this in a year? Whatever, the score was now: fish, two; Dan, zero.

I didn't come up with any answers, so I decided the best thing to do was to get out of the water, gather my composure and regroup before I made another feeble attempt at trying to catch a fish. So, I exited the water and went back to my favorite bench to await the sound of another familiar slurp. I listened intently and perused the river for any visible signs of fish feeding on the surface. For lack of nothing better to do, I took out my Mag-Lite and shined it across the river to see if there were any flies on the water. I could see several Spinners and a Hatcher now and then, so I decided to wait it out, at least until 11:30 p.m., which was an hour away.

Five minutes went by and no fish were feeding. Nine minutes went by and still no fish were feeding. As it approached 10:45 p.m. I heard a half-hearted slurp off to my right. It seemed to be coming from the middle of the river. I got up from my bench and walked to the river's edge, intently looking and listening for additional signs. I heard a second slurp from the same spot.

I decided to cautiously wade into the river to get a final location before I prepared for the anticipated battle. I didn't think much of the rise but decided to give it my all, considering that this might be my last shot at a fish for this evening.

As I was waiting I heard a third slurp, which came from directly in front of me, some twenty feet away, in the middle of the river. This time I noticed a significant movement of water (large V-shaped wake) after the fish fed. I concluded that it takes a fairly decent fish to move water like this when gathering in a fly. I got more serious about my plan of attack.

I ever so tenderly waded out into the river a little further, into knee-deep water, and positioned myself for a good cast and float over the fish. I stripped off about ten feet of line, which was about five feet short of where I saw the wake, and cast my fly to determine what type of float and drift I would get over the fish. (This was a practice I'd learned over the years and was something I usually did when fishing for a decent fish.)

Although I could barely see my fly, I knew I was getting a nice, long, natural float. The river was extremely wide and the current was not swift, as it was only about two-and-a-half feet deep. I now became very systematic about what I was going to do and how I would cast my fly.

I stripped off another five feet of line, cast my fly about ten feet above where the fish was feeding and mended my line for the expected natural float over the fish. As the fly got to the location where the fish was feeding, I heard a slurp so I picked up the rod tip, set the hook — and nothing happened. I began to think, "What the hell? Did I get snagged on a logjam or something else that floated down?" So, I reared back on the rod a little firmer — and all hell broke loose as I felt the thunderous, forceful tug of what I knew was a big fish.

The second set must have awakened the fish. It stripped off one hundred feet of line with a powerful run straight upriver in a matter of seconds. It took the line out so quickly out of my left hand and off the reel that it scorched my fingers as it went through. My first inclination was that I had to stop the fish before it got too far into my backing and broke off or tied me up in some logs or tag alders.

In an effort to stop it I pointed the butt section of my rod directly at the fish and applied pressure. It finally stopped, made a few sachets from side to side, took a few, short, sideward runs and then turned and made a second strong run downriver for about eighty or ninety feet. I pointed the butt section at the fish again. It stopped and proceeded across river to a logjam in an effort to tie me up and to break loose. I suspected that this was its homing ground, as it provided significant cover and excellent feed troughs.

I applied more pressure and it turned again. I called to Lucky and Mike for help, because I knew landing this fish might require more than one person. Not getting a response from them, I frantically gathered in some line so as not to slack it and give the fish the advantage of breaking off.

The fish then swam downriver for about fifty feet toward two cedar trees overhanging the river. I again applied pressure. It turned and came toward me, resting on the bottom of the river near the spot where I had hooked it. There it remained, sulking and constantly shaking its head from side to side in an attempt to gain freedom. It stayed there for what seemed like an eternity - although in reality it was probably only a minute. The battle had lasted fifteen minutes and I still didn't have the fish yet. At this time I used the old trick of thumping the bottom of the rod in the palm of my left hand, thereby transmitting vibrations to get the fish moving.

In over thirty-five years of fly-fishing I had fought several significant battles and two wars — but nothing as demanding as the full scale attack I was presently involved in. My worthy opponent used every trick it had gathered during its eight years plus of experience. This, by far, was the greatest war I had ever fought. This fight demanded every ounce of my energy and my constant attention. I was on the fish's battlefield, in its environment, which was not a very enviable position to be in.

Up to this point I wasn't sure who was going to outlast who or who was going to win the war. Victory was still up for grabs. I had never felt such power at the end of my rod before; never in all of my life.

Finally, after a second thump on the butt section of the rod, my opponent came to the surface and made a tremendous roll. It splashed water everywhere, as if a bomb had been dropped. I surmised that this was its last deliverance of everything in it arsenal before conceding defeat. It paused and came directly toward me.

This was my first opportunity to gain some ground in beginning to land the fish.

The fish seemed to be tiring so I began to retrieve my line - ten feet, fifteen feet, twenty feet, and more. It was now about eight to ten feet in front of me. As its shadow was cast against the bottom of the river in about ten inches of water I saw for the first time some evidence of its enormity. Apparently it was beginning to feel the effects of the tremendously powerful attack it had unleashed for the last twenty minutes. Victory was in sight, but not yet in hand.

It was now about five feet away, into my tippet. Comparing the size of my net versus the size of the fish, which I guessed to be about 25 inches, I knew it wouldn't fit. I decided not to try netting it for fear of losing this old-timer.

After retrieving the line about another foot, I made a split-second decision to put both hands on the rod and hoist the fish on shore (like a tuna), which I did with great success. Once the fish landed on shore, I dropped my rod, line and everything else and pounced on the fish as though it was a million dollars. In the process of securing the fish with my 250-pound torso I stepped on my rod and got tangled up in my line, but I managed to overcome these hurdles. It's amazing what you can do when there is a lot at stake. The battle lasted thirty minutes — even though it seemed like several hours had passed.

Upon seeing his size my only utterance was "Holy cow! What a trout!" I echoed these same words several times, in disbelief and shock over what had transpired.

As I picked him up to carry him further on shore the fly popped out of his mouth. So there is a lot to be said about always keeping tension and pressure on the fish by holding the rod tip high.

I had the catch of my lifetime solidly in my hands, even though he was making a few last ditch attempts to get free. I sat on the ground, hovering over my trophy until I could catch my breath and return my heart rate back to normal. I had the utmost respect and admiration for this great warrior.

Not having a tape or a scale, I relied on my past experience to make an educated guess about his weight and length. My guess was this hefty, hook-jawed male was 24 to 26 inches long and weighed between 6 and 7 pounds.

⚓

This experience was like a replay of when I caught a Big Brown on the Manistee River about ten years earlier. What an eerie feeling to have such a similar experience again. It's not often that one has the opportunity to catch a trophy fish - and for some unknown reason I had been blessed with the chance to catch three trophy fish during my forty years of trout fishing. The opportunity seems to arise about once every ten years.

The first time I caught a trophy fish was in the early seventies when I had the good fortune of catching a Brook Trout that was over 18 1/2 inches long and weighed 3 1/2 pounds. I was fishing the Clam River with my brother-in-law, Tom Klena (a long-time best friend and fishing buddy). Since then Tom and I have caught numerous Brookies between 12 and 16 inches. The last time we caught a large Brook Trout was in the early eighties when we simultaneously hooked identical 16-inch Brookies out of side-by-side culverts in the Clam River.

The second time I caught a trophy fish occurred in 1984. That's when I took the large, male Brown out of the Manistee River near the King Trout Ranch. He was about 25 inches long and weighed over five pounds.

The most recent trophy fish I caught was the one I took out of the Au Sable River. At a little more than 26 inches long and weighing approximately 7 pounds, he is the largest Brown I have caught — yet.

There isn't a day that goes by that I don't think of these three special events, if only for a brief moment. They have touched my life and heart forever and I will cherish them as long as I live. Money, status or prestige cannot begin to replace these treasured moments.

(I apologize for this short diversion but I felt it was important to digress. I'll now return to the conclusion of my most recent experience.)

⚜

After regaining my composure, I put the fish in my 14-inch creel (what a joke). His head and tail stuck out of each end! I walked downriver to where I could cross over to the other side. In order to secure my trophy, I put a death hold on him, uttering the words, "Please let me cross the river without losing my fish."

As I walked downriver I heard several fish feeding (probably on Hatchers), but I was too emotionally drained to care. My heart was still pounding. I was sweating profusely and felt extremely weak all over. I had my catch for the night. No, after a thirty-minute battle, I had my catch for the last forty years. This was more than enough for me.

As I crossed the river I kept saying to myself, "Hang onto the fish until you get across." Fortunately, I made it across without losing him.

I returned to my car; opened the trunk; took off my vest, waders and hat; broke down my rod; and placed everything in the trunk. I then took my prize catch out of the creel and placed it on top of my waders. He seemed to take up three-quarters of the trunk. I stared at the fish for about five minutes, still in disbelief of what had happened. I closed the trunk, opened the driver's side door and placed myself behind the wheel to await the return of Lucky and Mike. I was still weak and shaky.

While I waited I must have made five trips to the trunk to look at the fish. The reality of what had occurred hadn't yet registered.

I couldn't believe what I had done. It was truly a life-long dream come true. Fifteen minutes passed, but still no Lucky or Mike.

I turned on my headlights and sat for another fifteen minutes. Finally I heard them coming down the path. I got out of the car and greeted them. They asked why I had my headlights on. I responded that I was trying to give them a little more light so that they could see better. (Little did they know my motive was to have them come over to view my monster Brown.)

When I asked how they had done, they explained that they had nicked a few but hadn't caught anything. In turn, they asked how I had done. I said that I had stuck two and caught one fairly decent fish. (*Decent* meaning somewhere in the category of 17 to 20 inches.) They asked to see the fish.

We walked to the trunk and I slowly opened it. When they got their first glimpse of my catch their mouths dropped open and there was silence. Then I heard, "What a monster. That's one helluva fish. Where did you catch it? That's the biggest Brown I've ever seen!"

After admiring the fish for a couple of minutes, Lucky took out his ruler to measure it. It was slightly over 26 inches. We didn't have a scale, but we guessed it weighed between 6 1/2 and 7 pounds. We decided to go to Big Boy's for a celebration snack.

Upon arriving at Big Boy's, we took our seats and ordered what had come to be our customary late night/early morning snack: strawberry pie with vanilla ice cream and coffee. We stayed there for about an hour, during which time I probably relived my evening two or three more times. There is a strong camaraderie that exists between friends who are fly-fishermen. When someone catches a Big Brown there are genuine feelings of happiness shared all around.

It was about 1:30 a.m. by the time we were ready to leave Big Boy's. Lucky suggested that we go to Skip and Gail's to show them the fish. I suggested that it might be too late. Lucky said they wouldn't mind if we woke them up, so off we went to Skip and Gail's.

When we arrived at their home, I took my fish out of the trunk and the three of us went up to the house and knocked on the door. Fortunately they were still awake.

In we went. I placed my Brown on their countertop. They were in awe. They extended their heartfelt congratulations and we talked for awhile before deciding to leave.

Lucky took my fish to his house since the refrigerator in my motel room was too small. He said he would bring it into the Sport Shop the next morning. I finally got to bed about 3:15 a.m. but I couldn't fall asleep because the adrenaline was still pumping through my system. I couldn't stop thinking about what had happened.

I tossed and turned for about four hours, and I finally got out of bed about 7:30 a.m. I showered and shaved, then I went to the Lone Pine restaurant for breakfast, which was my usual routine. When I got to the Lone Pine, Marilyn and John asked me how I had done fishing the previous night. Boy, did I have a story for them! I again relived my evening. We reminisced about the trophy fish until 8:45 a.m.

After I left the Lone Pine I went to Skip's to tie flies until Lucky brought my prize catch to the shop.

Jack, Skip and Gail's son-in-law, was the only one at the shop when I arrived. He asked how I had done. I again relived the previous night. Jack was extremely happy for me. He had always hoped I would catch a trophy fish because I got so excited. Skip and Gail arrived about 9:30 a.m. I was still waiting for Lucky to bring my trophy. Finally he arrived about 10:15 a.m.

First Jack weighed the fish on the Sport Shop's scale. It weighed over 6 1/2 pounds but we figured it probably lost a half-pound between the time it was caught and the time we weighed it that morning. Then Skip and Gail got the largest ice cooler they had in the shop and filled it with ice. My fish was on display for the rest of the day.

The news of my fish spread like wildfire throughout the community. There was an onslaught of people who came to view it. All day long I rehashed my experience, to the minutest detail, with everyone who came into the shop. From the remarks I heard I felt like "King For A Day." I was overflowing with pride and joy. For many other Hex fishermen and me this was a fish of a lifetime. Most fishermen never catch a Big Brown over 20-inches — let alone a 26-incher.

This was life itself — and the true reality of what life was all about — at least for me. Catching this lunker was definitely my most memorable experience. If I hadn't caught another fish during the remaining two weeks of my vacation, it would have been okay with me because my season and life's work had all been wrapped up into that thirty-minute contest.

Yes, I had the fish mounted. Wouldn't you? My lifelong archrival now sits motionless, in full view, on the wall, always reminding me of that one special evening, "In the Thrill of the Night."

❦

I guess if there is any lesson to be learned from this experience it would be that you shouldn't pass up an opportunity, no matter what the size of the dimple, burp, slurp, gulp, etc. You never know what might lurk behind the smallest sound.

Chapter 5

TYING THE CATAU HEX

DURING THE SIXTIES I SPENT TWO YEARS CREATING THE CATAU HEX flies. This series of flies captures the May fly in its infancy through adulthood. I put the finishing touches on the final stage of the May fly while staying at Henderson's Lodge on the Au Sable River, several bends below Wakely Bridge. Henderson's Lodge was my home for three weeks every year when I fished the famous Michigan Hex hatch in late June and early July.

Additional credit for the Catau Hex must be given to my life-long friends and fishing buddies, Al Pretto and John Kennedy. Their suggestions and words of encouragement during the developmental stages of the flies were very helpful. Through their efforts I came up with the Dun and Spinner versions of the pattern as they exist today. With their input the flies' two long, hair-like tails progressed to one short, full tail; and their hackle wings changed to a white calf tail wing.

The design phase of the flies was filled with numerous trials and tribulations, and much research and development - both in the vise and on the rivers. The end results have proven to be two of the most effective "big fish getters" on the Au Sable and Manistee Rivers over the last thirty-five years.

In an article in the June 21, 1991 issue of the *Detroit Free Press*, Eric Sharp, outdoors writer, wrote: "Among the most effective "Hex" flies are Catau's Dun and Spinner patterns, which seek to present an attractive outline rather than a close imitation."

I share these patterns with you in hopes that they will bring you as much enjoyment and excitement as they have to many fisherpersons over the years while fishing the Hex hatch on these world class rivers. Fish these patterns religiously and they will fulfill your greatest expectations of catching Big Browns during the famed "Michigan Caddis Hatch."

CATAU'S HEX FLIES

Dun (Hatcher) Version

Hook: Mustad #9671, #9672 or equivalent
Size: #6 and #8
Thread: Yellow flat Monocord
Tail: White calf tail (full)
Rib: Either Grizzly or Brown Hackle palmered over body (long saddle hackle)
Body: Yellow, 4-strand yarn or polypropylene
Wing: Full clump of white calf tail tied upright
Hackle: Either two Grizzly or Brown Saddle Hackles tied parachute style

Steps for Tying

Step 1.   Tie in a full, short clump of white calf tail for the tail.

Step 2.   Tie in either one long quality Grizzly or Brown Saddle hackle, butt forward (let it hang).

Step 3.   Tie in yellow, 4-strand yarn or polypropylene for body and wrap forward toward eye, leaving enough room for calf tail wing and parachute hackle. Palmer the hackle tied in Step 2, the complete length of the body and stabilize.

Step 4.   Tie in a fairly long (1 to 1 1/4-inch) full, clump of white calf tail for wing (base of hair pointing back towards hook point). Apply a dab of head cement to area where hair was tied in. Wrap thread around hair 6 to 8 times to stabilize, then move thread to front of wing and wrap at base of clump to stand wing upright. Wrap around base of wing 6 to 8 times then move thread back behind wing.

Step 5. Tie in two, fairly long saddle hackles (good quality) behind wings with butt section forward. These saddles should be the same color as those used for palmered ribbing. Hackles should lie flat along the top of the body. Grab the first hackle tip with your pliers and wrap around base of upright wing, horizontally towards eye of hook. Wrap 5 or 6 turns and stabilize. Repeat the same process with the second hackle. Wrap thread around hook in conventional manner to make head. Half-hitch or whip finish and cement head.

Spinner (Spent) Version

Hook: Mustad #9671, #9672 or equivalent

Size: #6 or #8

Thread: Yellow flat Monocord

Tail: White calf tail (full)

Rib: Either Grizzly or
Brown hackle palmered over
body

Body: Yellow, wool yarn or
polypropylene

Wing: Full, white calf tail tied spent (slightly forward)

Hackle: Either Grizzly or Brown, tied conventional style

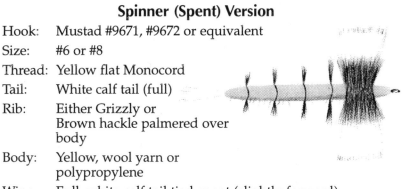

Steps for Tying

Step 1. Tie in a short, full, clump of white calf tail for tail.

Step 2. Tie in either one long, quality Grizzly or Brown Saddle hackle, butt first (let it hang).

Step 3. Tie in yellow wool yarn (4-strand) or polypropylene for body and wrap forward toward eye of hook, leaving enough room for calf tail wing, conventional hackle and head of fly. Palmer the hackle tied in Step 2, the complete length of body and stabilize.

Step 4.   Tie in a fairly long (approximately 2 to 2 1/4 inches) full, clump of white calf tail for wing. (Base of hair pointing back towards hook point.) Apply a dab of head cement to where calf tail was tied in. Stabilize with 5 or 6 turns. Separate calf tail into equal parts on each side of hook shank. Use a figure eight movement around each separate wing for 6 or 7 turns until wings separate in a spent fashion. Cock wings slightly forward by moving thread in back of wings and making several wraps at base. Stabilize.

Step 5.   Tie in two, fairly long Grizzly or Brown saddle hackles (good quality) behind wings, with butt sections forward. These saddle hackles should be the same color as the one used for the palmered ribbing. Hackles should be tied in at about a 60-degree angle to hook shank. Grab the first hackle tip with your pliers and wrap hackle conventionally around shank, behind wings about three times, then wrap around the shank in front of wings three times and stabilize. Repeat same process with second hackle. Wrap thread around hook to make head. Half hitch or whip finish and cement head.

These Hex patterns are excellent floaters because of the palmering over the body and the quality of hackle used for the parachute and spent wing versions. The tail is tied short to cause the fly to ride lower in the water at the rear end. This will enhance your capability to hook fish easier because the rod tip doesn't have to be moved drastically to set the hook. Tied properly and tightly it will result in a very durable fly, which will produce several fish before requiring changing. Try them. I think you will like them.

Catau Brown Drake

Hook: #9671 or #9672
Size: #10, #12
Head: Black or brown thread
Tail: Two long barbules off a Pheasant tail
Body: 4 to 5 long Pheasant tail barbules
Hackle: Two furnace-brown hackles
Wing: Two furnace-brown hackle points

Steps for Tying

Step 1. Tie in two, long Pheasant tail barbules (butts first at end of hook).

Step 2. Tie in 4 or 5 reddish brown, variegated Pheasant tail barbules in front of tail (butts first).

Step 3. Run thread to where you tie in two furnace-brown hackle points for either upright or spent wings (butts first) and secure.

Step 4. Wrap the 4 or 5 Pheasant tail barbules toward wings to create a reddish-brown, variegated body. Secure body in front of wings.

Step 5. Tie in two dark furnace-brown, dry fly hackles behind wings (butts first). Wrap each hackle individually toward eye of hook. Make three turns behind wings and two turns in front of wings. Secure hackle quills.

Step 6. Create head - either half hitch or whip finish.

Step 7. Apply head cement over complete head.

Catau Little Yellow Stone

Hook: #94840 Mustad

Size: #14 or #16

Tail: None

Body: Yellow polypropylene

Wing: Bronze wood duck tied trude over top of body

Hackle: Two medium-brown dry fly hackles

Head: Yellow flat Monocord

Steps for Tying

Step 1. Tie in yellow polypropylene and wrap forward towards eye of hook - make body fairly plump and tapered. Secure body. Make sure to leave enough room for the trude wing over body and hackle to create a nice clean head.

Step 2. Cut off a medium portion of bronze wood duck barbules from one single wood duck feather. Tie in barbules so that they extend over the body to a little past bend in hook. Secure wing.

Step 3.   Tie in two medium-brown dry fly hackles in front of trude wing. Wrap each individual hackle about 3 or 4 turns in front of wing and secure.

Step 4.   Create head and half hitch or whip finish.

Step 5.   Apply head cement over complete head.

Michigan Hopper

Hook: #9672 Mustad

Size: #8 or #10

Tail: Short, red duck quill, calf tail or floss cut to size

Body: Either medium-yellow, green or brown chenille

Wing: Clump of medium-brown deer hair tied trude over body

Hackle: Two medium-dark-brown, dry fly Saddle hackles (good quality)

Head: Black or yellow flat Monocord

Steps for Tying

Step 1.   Tie in a short red tail (tag) of either duck quill, calf tail or floss cut to size.

Step 2.   Tie in medium-yellow, green or brown chenille in front of tag and wrap forward to where a clump of brown deer hair will be tied in trude over body. Secure chenille.

Step 3.   Tie in a clump of brown deer hair, butts first, trude over body to where it extends just beyond bend of hook. Apply a dab of head cement on deer hair and secure with several wraps of thread.

Step 4.   Tie in two medium-brown dry fly saddle hackles on top of where deer hair is secured. Wrap each individual hackle toward eye of hook and secure. Hackle should be in front of deer hair.

Step 5.   Wrap thread to make head and finish off with either half hitches or whip finish.

Step 6.   Apply head cement to head.

EFFECTIVE FLY PATTERNS FOR
FISHING THE MANISTEE & AU SABLE RIVERS

A full color guide of the fly patterns that have proven to be effective in fishing the Manistee and Au Sable Rivers.

ADAMS

BLACK ANT

SPENT WING BORCHERS

CATAU'S BROWN DRAKE

CADDIS PUPA (NYMPH)

CATAU'S MAY FLY (HEX) - DUN

CATAU'S MAY FLY (HEX) - SPENT

CINNAMON ANT

COACHMAN

COACHMAN (STREAMER)

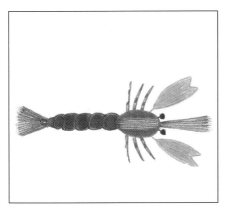

CATAU'S CRAYFISH

DARK HENDRICKSON

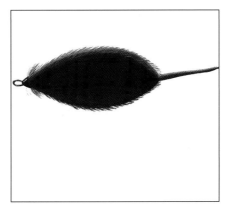

CATAU'S DEER HAIR MOUSE

DRY SKUNK

ELK HAIR CADDIS

HARES EAR NYMPH

HUMPY

HUMPY

LETORT CRICKET

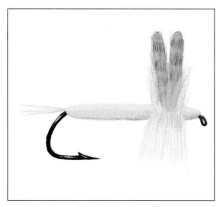

LIGHT CAHILL

LIGHT HENDRICKSON

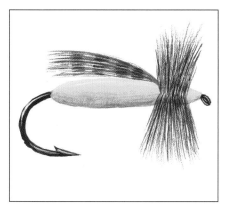

CATAU'S LITTLE YELLOW STONE

**CATAU'S MAY FLY
(DUN) - HATCHER**

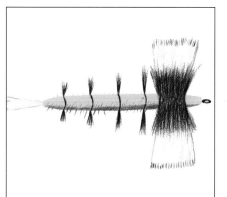

**CATAU'S MAY FLY
(SPINNER) - SPENT**

MICHIGAN HOPPER

MICKEY FINN

MUDDLER MINNOW

PICKET PINN

QUILL GORDON

ROBERT'S DRAKE

ROYAL COACHMAN

ROYAL COACHMAN (STREAMER)

CATAU'S SMALL HOPPER

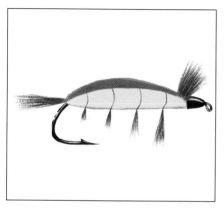

SPRING WIGGLER (WEIGHTED)

CATAU'S TRIMMED DEER HAIR
MAY FLY

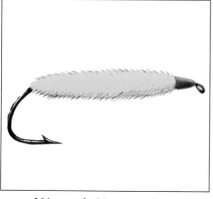

WAKELY'S YELLOW BUG

WET SKUNK

 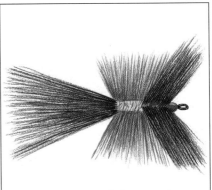

CATAU'S WHEAT SHUCK MAY FLY (HEX) IMITATION

Wet Skunk (Weighted)

Hook: Mustad #9672 or equivalent (long shank)

Size: #2, #4, #6, #8 and #10

Tail: White calf tail

Body: Medium-black chenille wrapped over .20 or .25 lead wire

Legs: Three pair of medium white rubber legs tied over black chenille

Head: Flat black Monocord

Steps for Tying

Step 1.   Tie in a short, medium clump of white calf tail at bend of hook.

Step 2.   Tie in a long piece of medium black chenille and let hang.

Step 3.   Tie in .20 or .25 lead wire and wrap around hook shank toward eye. Stabilize lead by running thread up to eye of hook, back to bend of hook and back to eye.

Step 4.   Wrap black chenille over lead complete length of body, toward eye of hook. Secure body.

Step 5.   Run thread from eye of hook toward bend of hook. Tie in one pair of rubber legs. Work forward and tie in second and third pair of rubber legs. Figure eight legs to make them stand outwardly. End up with thread at eye of hook.

Step 6.   Wrap thread and make head. Secure with 3 or 4 half hitches or whip finish.

Step 7.   Apply head cement to complete head.

Tie unweighted Skunk in the exact same manner minus the lead wrapped around the hook shank.

Dry Skunk

Hook: Mustad #9672 or equivalent (long shank)

Size: #2, #4, #6, #8 and #10

Tail: White calf tail

Body: Medium-black chenille

Wing: Medium-brown deer hair

Legs: Two pair of medium white rubber legs

Hackle: Two medium-brown hackle points

Head: Flat-black Monocord

Steps for Tying

Step 1.   Tie in a short, medium clump of white calf tail at bend of hook.

Step 2.   Tie in a long piece of medium-black chenille and wrap toward eye of hook, where body will end, and secure.

Step 3.   Run thread back toward bend in hook and tie in one pair of rubber legs. Run thread forward and tie in another pair of rubber legs. (A third pair of rubber legs is optional.)

Step 4.   Run thread forward to where body was secured and tie in a medium clump of deer hair (butts forward) and secure. Place a dab of head cement where deer hair was secured and make several additional wraps around the deer hair. (This is done to ensure that the individual deer hair fibers don't pull out.)

Step 5.   Tie in two fairly long, medium-brown, dry fly saddle hackles (butts forward on about a 60-degree angle). Wrap each hackle individually towards eye of hook and secure.

Step 6.   Wrap thread and make head. Secure with 3 or 4 half hitches or whip finish.

Step 7.   Apply head cement to complete head.

The Famed Robert's Drake

Hook: #9671 or #9672 Mustad

Size: #12, #14 or #16

Tail: Pheasant tail barbules

Body: Brown deer hair
         wrapped over
         shank of hook

Wing: White calf tail or deer hair

Hackle: Two medium-brown hackles

Head: Flat yellow Monocord

Steps for Tying

Step 1.   Tie in several Pheasant tail barbules, medium length, and secure. Run thread toward eye of hook where body will be ending.

Step 2.   Tie in a medium clump of brown deer hair, butts toward eye, and secure. Leave a small tuft of deer hair in front of body that will require clipping. Wrap yellow flat Monocord from where you secured deer hair back towards bend of hook and then back towards eye of hook where you first secured the deer hair. Make sure wraps of thread are firm over deer hair body. Leave a small tuft of deer hair at the back end of the body over the Pheasant tail barbules. Clip excess deer hair from the front of the body.

Step 3.   Tie in a clump of either white calf tail or deer hair, tips forward, and secure. Place a small dab of head cement on hair where it is tied in. Move thread to front of wing and make 5 or 6 turns at base of hair to stand wing upright. Move thread to behind upright wing and make 5 or 6 turns over head-cemented area. Secure all material.

Step 4.   Tie in two medium-brown, dry fly hackles, butts first, so they lay parallel over body. Wrap each hackle individually around upright wing in a parachute fashion and secure.

Step 5.   Wrap thread to make head and finish off with 3 or 4 half hitches or whip finish.

Step 6.   Apply head cement.

Chapter 6

EFFECTIVE FLY PATTERNS

CATAU'S MAY FLY (DUN) HATCHER

CATAU'S MAY FLY (SPINNER) SPENT

(Hex)		(Hex)	
Hook:	#9671 or #9672 Mustad	Hook:	#9671 or #9672 Mustad
Size:	#4, #6 or #8	Size:	#4, #6 or #8
Thread:	Yellow	Thread:	Yellow
Tail:	White calf tail	Tail:	White calf tail
Body:	4-strand yellow yarn or polypropylene palmered with either a brown or grizzly hackle	Body:	4-strand yellow yarn or polypropylene palmered with either a brown or grizzly hackle
Wing:	Upright white calf tail	Wing:	Spent white calf tail
Hackle:	Either brown or grizzly	Hackle:	Either brown or grizzly

CATAU'S
BROWN DRAKE

Hook: #9671 or #9672 Mustad

Size: #10 or #12

Thread: Black or brown Monocord

Tail: Two long Pheasant tail barbules

Body: 4 or 5 long Pheasant tail barbules

Wing: Two furnace-brown hackle points

Hackle: Two furnace-brown hackles

CATAU'S
LITTLE YELLOW STONE

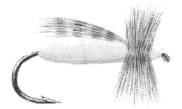

Hook: #94840 Mustad

Size: #12, #14 or #16

Thread: Yellow Monocord

Body: Yellow polypropylene

Wing: Bronze wood duck

Hackle: Two medium-brown hackles

MICHIGAN HOPPER

Hook   #9671 Mustad

Size: #8 or #10

Thread: Yellow Monocord

Tail: Short red duck quill, calf tail or floss cut to size

WET SKUNK

Hook: #9672, #9675 Mustad or equivalent

Size: #2, #4, #6, #8 or #10

Thread: Black Monocord

Tail: White calf tail

Body: Medium-black chenille

Body: Either medium-brown, yellow or green chenille

Wing: Medium-brown deer hair

Hackle: Two medium-dark-brown dry fly hackles

Underbody: .20 or .25 lead

Legs: Three pair of medium white rubber legs

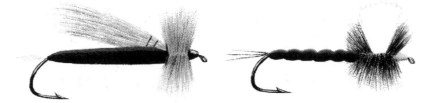

DRY SKUNK

ROBERT'S DRAKE

Hook: #9672 Mustad

Size: #2, #4, #6, #8 or #10

Thread: Black monocord

Tail: White calf tail

Body: Medium-black chenille

Legs: Two pairs of medium-white rubber legs

Wing: Light-brown deer hair

Hackle: Two medium-brown hackle points

Hook: #9671 Mustad

Size: #10, #12, #14 or #16

Thread: Yellow monocord

Tail: Pheasant tail barbules

Body: Light-brown deer hair

Wing: White calf tail

Hackle: Two medium-brown hackle points

ELK HAIR CADDIS

Hook: #9671 Mustad

Size: #10, #12, #14 or #16

Thread: Yellow Monocord

Body: Light-tan natural fur
         dubbing, palmered with
         brown hackle

Wing: Elk hair tied trude

ADAMS

Hook: #94840 Mustad

Size: #10, #12, #14 or #16

Thread: Black Monocord

Tail: Grizzly hackle barbules

Body: Gray muskrat dubbed

Hackle: One grizzly and one
         brown, mixed

CATAU'S MAY FLY (HEX) DUN

Hook: #9672 Mustad

Size: #2, #4, #6 or #8

Thread: Yellow Monocord

Tail: Two Pheasant tail barbules

Body: Deer hair (medium)

CATAU'S MAY FLY (HEX) SPENT

Hook: #9672 Mustad

Size: #2, #4, #6 or #8

Thread: Yellow Monocord

Tail: Two Pheasant tail bar-
         bules

Body: Deer hair (medium)

Wing: Either grizzly or brown hackle points

Hackle: Either grizzly or brown hackle

Wing: Two pairs of either grizzly or brown hackle points

Hackle: Either grizzly or brown hackle

SPENT WING BORCHERS

CATAU'S SMALL HOPPER

Hook: #94840 Mustad

Size: #10, #12, #14 or #16

Thread: Black Monocord

Tail: Pheasant tail barbules

Body: Light-oak turkey quill wrapped around shank

Wing: Bluish-lavender

Hackle: Bluish-lavender

Hook: #9671 Mustad

Size: #10, #12 or #14

Thread: Yellow Monocord

Tail: Red calf tail or floss cut to size

Body: Yellow yarn palmered with brown hackle

Wing: Light-brown deer hair

CATAU'S TRIMMED DEER HAIR MAY FLY

Hook:	#9672 Mustad
Size:	#2, #4, #6 or #8
Thread:	Yellow Monocord
Tail:	Pheasant tail barbules
Body:	Medium-brown trimmed deer hair
Wing:	Grizzly hackle points
Hackle:	Two grizzly hackles

LIGHT CAHILL

Hook:	#94840 Mustad
Size:	#10, #12, #14 or #16
Thread:	Yellow or cream Monocord
Tail:	Cream hackle fibers
Body:	Cream dubbing
Wing:	Bronze wood duck
Hackle:	Two cream hackles

LIGHT HENDRICKSON

Hook:	#94840 Mustad
Size:	#12 or #14
Thread:	Brown
Tail:	Medium dun hackle fibers
Body:	Pale pinkish/brown fox fur or synthetic substitute
Wing:	Wood duck fibers
Hackle:	Medium-blue dun

DARK HENDRICKSON

Hook:	#94840 Mustad
Size:	#12, #14, #16 or #18
Thread:	Gray
Tail:	Dark dun cock hackle fibers
Body:	Dark muskrat or synthetic substitute
Wing:	Wood duck fibers
Hackle:	Dark blue dun

COACHMAN

Hook: #94840 Mustad
Size: #10, #12, #14 or #16
Thread: Black
Tail: Golden pheasant tippets
Body: Peacock herl
Wing: White hackle points
Hackle: Furnace brown hackle points

ROYAL COACHMAN

Hook: #94840 Mustad
Size: #10, #12, #14 or #16
Thread: Black
Tail: Golden pheasant tippets
Body: Tuft of peacock herl, red floss in middle, tuft of peacock herl
Wing: White hackle points

Hackle: Furnace-brown hackle points

PICKET PIN

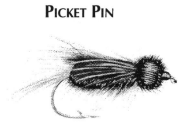

Hook: #9672 Mustad
Size: #8 - #12
Thread: Black
Tail: Brown cock hackle fibers

QUILL GORDON

Hook: #94840 Mustad
Size: #10 - #18
Thread: Cream or light. brown
Tail: Medium-blue dun cock hackle fibers

Body:	Peacock herl, palmered with brown hackle fibers
Wing:	Gray squirrel tail
Head:	Peacock herl

Body:	Stripped peacock quill
Wing:	Wood duck
Hackle:	Medium-blue dun cock hackle

WAKELY'S YELLOW BUG

Hook:	#9672 Mustad
Size:	#10 - #14
Thread:	Yellow
Body:	Either trimmed yellow deer hair or deer hair wrapped around shank

BLACK OR CINNAMON ANT

Hook:	#94840 Mustad
Size:	#14 - #18
Thread:	Black or brown
Body:	Either black or cinnamon dubbing
Hackle:	Black or brown

LETORT CRICKET

Hook:	#9671 or #9672 Mustad
Size:	#8 - #14
Thread:	Black

MICKEY FINN

Hook:	#9675 Mustad
Size:	#2 - #10
Thread:	Black

Body: Black dubbing or Polypropylene

Wing: Black goose quill

Head: Trimmed, black deer hair

Collar: Black deer hair left unclipped

Body: Flat silver tinsel overlaid with oval silver tinsel

Wing: Yellow buck tail, red buck tail in the middle and yellow buck tail on top

Head: Build up - painted black with yellow eye

Hares Ear Nymph

Hook: #9671 Mustad

Size: #10 - #14

Tail: Hare body fur

Body: Hare fur dubbed on hook

Hackle: Hare fur fibers picked out

Wing case: Black feather fiber

Thorax: Hare fur

Caddis Pupa (Nymph)

Hook: Caddis type

Size: #8 - #12

Thread: Black

Body: Medium-green larvae lace or swanundaze

Collar: Peacock herl tied in at top and bottom

Head: peacock herl wrapped around to create large head

COACHMAN (STREAMER)

ROYAL COACHMAN (STREAMER)

Hook: #9672 - #9675 Mustad
Size: #2 - #14
Thread: Black
Tail: Golden pheasant tippets
Body: Peacock herl

Wing: Either white calf tail or two hackle points

Hackle: Furnace-brown, tied under wing

Hook: #9672 - #9675 Mustad
Size: #2 - #14
Thread: Black
Tail: Golden pheasant tippets
Body: Peacock herl, red floss in middle, peacock herl

Wing: Either white calf tail or two hackle points

Hackle: Furnace-brown tied under wing

MUDDLER MINNOW

SPRING WIGGLER (WEIGHTED)

Hook: #9672 or #9675 Mustad
Size: #2 - #12
Thread: Black

Hook: #9672 Mustad
Size: #4 - #10
Thread: Black

Tail:	Oak turkey slip	Tail:	Fox squirrel tail formed by overbody
Body:	Gold tinsel		
Hackle:	Collar of unclipped deer hair	Underbody:	.20 lead wrapped around shank
Wing:	Gray squirrel tail with oak turkey slips (either side)	Body:	Either yellow, hot orange or chartreuse
Head:	Clipped deer hair	Overbody:	Fox squirrel tail extended over body and ends clipped to size
		Hackle:	Medium-Brown palmered over body

CATAU'S CRAYFISH

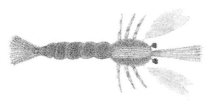

HUMPY

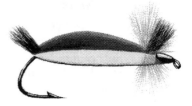

Hook:	Extra long shank
Size:	#0x, #2, #4 or #6
Thread:	Amber or medium-brown
Fan tail:	Moose mane
Underbody:	.25 lead, wrapped full length of shank from front to back and halfway toward front. Moose mane full length of shank, over lead.
Body:	Amber swanundaze or larvae lace
Head:	Medium-brown chenille
Eyes:	30 lb. monofilament, melted

Hook:	9672 Mustad or Equivalent
Size:	#6, #8, #10, or #12
Tail:	Clump of medium-brown deer hair left extended from wing case over body
Body:	Either yellow or red 4-strand floss
Wing Case:	Medium-brown deer hair tied in at back of fly and pulled tightly over body to eye of hook. Leave a small clump of deer hair extended over eye of hook.

Pincers:	Light-tan pheasant breast feathers, vinyl cemented	Hackle:	One grizzly and one medium-brown tied in
Legs:	Dark- brown mottled pheasant flank, feathers separated and cemented		butts first and wrapped conventionally around hook.
Feelers:	Moose mane	Head:	Flat-black monocord

CATAU'S WHEAT SHUCK
MAY FLY (HEX) IMITATION

Hook: #9672 or #9575 Mustad or Equivalent

Size: #4, #6 or #8

Body: Four-strand Yellow Yarn or Polypropolene

Ribbing: One medium-brown hackle palmered over body

Rear Wing: Clump of medium-brown deer hair tied trude over rear half of body

Middle Hackle: Two medium-brown saddle hackles tied in and wrapped conventionally at middle of the fly

Front Wing: Clump of medium-brown deer hair tied spent with wings slightly cocked forward

Front Hackle: Two medium-brown saddle hackles tied in behind wing and wrapped conventionally to in front of wing

Head: Flat black or brown monocord

CATAU'S DEER HAIR MOUSE

Hook: #9672 or #9575 Mustad or Equivalent

Size: #2, #4, #6 or #8

Tail: Piece of deer hide cut and trimmed to represent tail of mouse

Body: Course deer hair flared, spun on the hook and packed tightly all the way to eye of hook. After making head and whip finishing or half-hitching, remove fly from vise and trim deer hair to form body of mouse, leaving two deer hair projections about 3/8 of an inch long at head (one on each side) to represent ears of mouse. Trim underside of body close to allow for hook exposure and hooking power.

Head: Flat black monocord

Chapter 7

CREATE YOUR OWN HEX PATTERNS

IF YOU FEEL SO INCLINED AND HAVE MASTERED SEVERAL BASIC fundamental fly-tying skills, creating your own Hex pattern(s) can be a very rewarding experience - especially if it produces the desired result — catching a Big Brown on the Manistee, Au Sable and other rivers and streams of northern Michigan. During the Michigan Caddis Hatch large Browns, Brookies and Rainbows feed abundantly on the larvae (Wigglers) and adult stages of this fly. From all assessments, this hatch is the peak time of the feeding cycle for all trout. This annual hatch represents the culmination of all hatches during the fly-fishing season. It is the only hatch that has the ability to draw out large trout that may never be seen or heard at any other time. Granted, some good bait fisherman may take large trout (twenty-plus inches) during the season on crawlers or minnows, but never in the quantities that this hatch produces year after year.

So, you see, creating your own hex pattern(s) can be a very worthwhile adventure. When making your Hex pattern of choice, remember to follow these basic guidelines:

- ❋ Use a hook size (6 and 8 with 2x and 3x shanks) preferably in the dry fly category that represents the actual size of the May fly (1 to 11/2 inches), both Dun and Spinner versions, and provides a good silhouette on the water at night for feeding trout.

- ❋ Use materials with good floatability for the tail, body and wings as the Hex rides high on the water's surface.

- ❋ Use colors that simulate those found on the actual May fly.

- ❋ Leave enough room at the eye of the hook to make a nice head so that you don't have to fight excessive material in the eye, which can be very restrictive when fishing at night.

- ❋ Tie a durable and tight fly to avoid disintegration of the fly when false casting or catching a fish.

- ❋ Keep the eye free and clear of head cement.

- ❋ Insure that the artificial fly is in proportion to the actual fly.

Once you have accomplished the above, the last order of business is to perform a little research and development by testing the fly(s) during a night of Hex fishing. Make sure you take along a few proven conventional patterns to use, should your pattern(s) prove to be ineffective. You don't want to get caught short-handed, especially if the fish begin to feed.

If your pattern(s) don't work, I suggest you continue to mix and match additional variations until you find one that does the job by catching a trout. This might require several sessions of research and development, but take it from me, it's all well worth the effort when you come up with the right combination. Once you catch a large trout on your pattern you will begin to reap the benefits. Trust me, there are no better feelings than those feelings resulting from personal accomplishment and creativity.

Good luck on creating your personal Hex pattern(s).

AFTERWORD

If you happen to be in Grayling, Michigan during the last two weeks of June, stop in at Skip's Sport Shop (located approximately one mile from the main four corners in town, west on M-72 on the left). You can't miss it, as there is a large sign out front.

Skip and Gail are very personable and gracious hosts. And, they are willing to share information pertaining to the Hex hatch, i.e., whether or not it is occurring and if so, where. They will also tell you how to locate the best fishing spots on the Au Sable and Manistee rivers. (Their son-in-law, Jack, is very adept at the sport of bow and rifle hunting. He is willing to share his expertise in that field.)

If you arrive early enough, you might be able to get a free cup of coffee and a donut or two. Late comers have to buy and bring their own.

I'll also be there, doing my usual - tying flies all day and fishing at night. If you need a refresher course in fly-fishing or fly-tying my services are there for the asking, at no cost I might add. (Highly unusual in today's market.)

County maps of both rivers are available at no cost. Whatever your fishing needs, I'm sure Skip's has it. Just ask. Their inventory is overflowing with the equipment you'll need for night fishing, including a large selection of rods, reels, waders, flies, fly lines, nets, tippets, flash lights and clothing. Or if you prefer to come in and browse or to exchange fishing stories, feel free to do so.

I invite you to visit one of the famous gathering spots in the north. I'm sure you will be pleased with what you see and get.

I look forward to seeing you soon!

Jack Nicklaus

August 30, 1991

Appendix

Dear Dan:

    I have been on the road almost non-stop lately, but when I returned home yesterday, I was delighted to find your flies awaiting me, along with your nice letter and the newspaper article. The flies are impressive, and I'm eager to put them to the test.

    I enjoyed meeting you and am glad we had the chance to chat. Maybe one of these days I'll be able to take you up on your invitation to fish the Ausable; in the meantime, I wish you all the best.

    Thanks again for thinking of me.

Best regards,

Mr. Dan J. Catau
Post Office Box 738
New Baltimore, MI 48047

/mk

11780 U. S. Highway #1, North Palm Beach, Florida 33408

Michigan river produces whopper

By Eric Sharp
Detroit Free Press
Sunday, August 3, 1997

Grayling, Mich. -- It looked more like a muskellunge, a dark-spotted killer that made its living gobbling down hapless smaller brethren.

But Gail Madsen's fish was clearly a brown trout, and still lodged in the jaw of the 30-inch, 10 1/4-pound behemoth was the dry fly she used to catch it on the Manistee River.

When Madsen brought the giant into Skip's Sport Shop the morning after she caught it, her brother, Mel Lucksted, laid next to it some trout he had hooked. "That's not fair," he said. "Some of those nice trout, 18-inchers, and that thing makes them look like minnows."

Madsen was fishing with her husband, Skip Madsen, her partner in the store where Dan Catau, a safety supervisor for Chrysler Corp. in Detroit, spends a chunk of his vacation to tie flies during the annual hatch of the Hexagenia limbata mayflies (and fishes for big trout at night).

North America's biggest mayfly hatches in late June and early July, bringing out mobs of anglers to night fish for big cannibal trout that normally don't feed much on insects but love to gorge these juicy morsels.

Madsen was using Catau's favorite hex imitation. It has white calf hair tail and semi-spent wings, a yellow body, and a furnace feather palmer-wrapped up the body to form the hackle. He mostly ties it on No. 6 hooks.

It floats well, matches the size of the natural fly and the color of a hex's belly and is as visible to the angler in the dark as it is to the fish.

Rusty Gates, who owns the Au Sable Lodge, said the biggest fish he has caught on a fly or has seen caught was 25 inches, "and in these rivers 5 pounds is a lot for a fish that size. There's just not the food base for them to grow faster."

The Madsens hadn't been on the river very long that night when they slid their Au Sable boat down a stretch of the Manistee where Skip and a friend had spooked a very big fish about 11:30 the night before.

"The spinner fall (adults returning to hatch) had just started, and the fish was there," Gail said. "I saw him feed a couple of times below us, and Skip said he wanted to ease the boat down another 10 feet to give me a better angle. We stopped about 25 feet away. I watched a spinner drift down toward him, and when he rose to take it, it looked like 40 gallons of water bulged up."

She had already stripped out the line needed for the cast and had it lying in the bottom of the boat. She false-cast the line and dropped the fly onto the water about a foot above where the trout rose.

"I wanted to drop it near him because I didn't want him to have time to look it over,"she said. "If you watch hex spinners, you'll see they just kind of plop down onto the water, so I wasn't worried about spooking him. He took it right away.

"I knew he was big, but when he made the first run he took out all of my line and a chunk of the backing. I've never had a trout do that in the river before."

It took 35 minutes to land the fish as it made repeated runs upstream and down, doggedly refusing to come to the net. She couldn't pressure it because the 5X leader had a breaking strength of about 4 pounds.

Madsen has caught a lot of big trout in her life, but nothing like this. The big brown was probably 8-10 years old and, because of its size, it looked like the closely related Atlantic salmon or one of the migratory, oceangoing browns that the English call sea trout.

Overall, the hex hatch, which probably will be over when you read this, saw more big trout caught than the two or three years preceding it, mostly from the Manistee and the south branch of the Au Sable.

But even if you didn't catch a fish half as long as Madsen's, don't give up. The crowds will melt away now, and some of the season's best dry fly fishing can be had in late July and August if you fish early and late — and find stretches of river where the trout see a lot of terrestrials.

And where there's one monster like hers, there has to be another, and we might just luck into it.

Don't laugh. Believing that is what makes us anglers.

Gloop, gloop means great hex fishing time

ERIC SHARP

Outdoors

GRAYLING — "Gloop."

The sound comes from the dark waters of the Manistee River, maybe 20 feet upstream, about the same place from where a bat came a couple of minutes earlier.

But I've never heard a bat go "gloop" and I've never seen one in the water, although I have hooked a few out of the air when they hit dry flies I was false-casting.

No, the sound marks a trout feeding, which is why Al Paulsen of Detroit and I are stumbling around in the Manistee an hour after dark.

The first good hatch of giant Hexegenia limbata mayflies

it, and a couple of seconds later 24 inches of black-spotted, red-dotted, yellow-bellied brown trout gleam in the meshes as we shine our lights on it.

"Geez, that's the biggest trout I ever caught in Michigan," Paulsen says, his breath as short as if he'd just run a mile. He takes the net from my hand and reaches in with a forceps to twist the fly out of the fish's mouth.

"I swear this is harder to do every time," he says as he hesitates, then decants the fish into the stream. He supports it in his hand for a minute, head to the current, then it scoots off with a tail flip that soaks Paulsen's face.

I know four other people who have caught brown trout of 22 inches or better on dry flies in the past few nights, the biggest a 26-inch, 6-pounder caught by Dan Catau.

A safety specialist at the Detroit Chrysler plant, Catau spends two weeks in Grayling during the hex several very big fish every year.

Bill Tichenell of Illyria, Ohio, spends a week of his vacation in Grayling every summer at hex time, checking in at The Fly Factory and Gates' Au Sable Lodge each day, where he listens to the stories from the night before. He then tries to separate the wheat from the chaff to help him decide where to fish that night.

"This year I got a 24-incher about a mile downstream from Mio the second night I was here," Tichenell said.

"I was sitting in my car in the parking lot at The Fly Factory, looking at a map, when two guys stopped by my back bumper to talk. One complained he hadn't seen a decent hatch, and his buddy kind of whispered where there had been a good hatch the night before.

"I didn't have any better ideas, so I went there that night about 10:30, waded out by a slow bend and waited. In 3½ hours I caught that 24-incher and four other fish, all of them 17 inches or bigger," he said.

Hex fishing is both tedious, because it sometimes involves long hours of waiting for hatches that never materialize, and exciting, because there is nothing quite like the anticipation of standing in a river and listening to the sound of big trout feeding all around

In the few minutes it takes me to wade carefully upstream, Paulsen brings the fish to within 10 feet, where it still fights gamely and circles him.

As it comes around again, it blunders into the net I'm holding in front of

other friend who _____ has been watching it for a week, and we're hoping tonight will bring another hatch and a spinner fall.

The good hex hatches started on most of the Au Sable in late June, about two weeks past the usual time.

Nights have been warm and muggy, ideal hex weather, and if things continue that way there should be excellent hatches right through the coming weekend on streams all over northern Michigan.

A tiny light gleams 150 yards upstream. Paulsen is changing flies or checking his leader or something.

Measuring out about 25 feet of line, I drop the fly at what I figure is about three feet above the "gloop." There's a big tree trunk sunk in a deep pool there, although I can't see it now.

Nothing happens on the first cast, but on the second there's a splash and a hard tug on the line as I raise the rod in reaction to the sound.

It's a decent fish, but before I can say anything, Paulsen whoops from upstream and yells, "I've got Moby Brown!" As I bring in and release an 18-inch brown, Paulsen is yelling, "Bring a net. I forgot my bleeping net and I'm going to lose this bleeper. It's as strong as a horse."

Detroit Free Press

Dan Catau of North Lakeport lured this 22-inch brown trout with a Hexagenia limbata imitation he tied.

ERIC SHARP
Detroit Free Press

It's a hatch to tie for

BY ERIC SHARP
Free Press Outdoors Writer

GRAYLING — Living in Grayling, you would think an angler could hit the famous hex hatch right on the money every night.

"I've been out six times, and I haven't hit a good night yet," grumps Steve Southard, owner of the Fly Factory. "Every time we went, the flies just weren't hatching where we were. Then the first night I had to work late at the store, my dad (Hal) called and said, 'There's a great hatch on. They're all over the screen door.' He had a great night, but I couldn't go. I'll be out again tonight, though."

Dan Catau, a Chrysler Corp. health and safety specialist who lives in North Lakeport, was at the right place at the right time two nights out of three. The first night produced a string of 15- to 18-inch fish, topped by a 20½-incher. The third saw him take only one fish, a 22-inch beauty that most fly fishermen only dream about.

"I saw it feeding two nights in a row at 12:05," said Catau, who also ties flies commercially and spends two weeks each year in Grayling during this hatch. "I was there at 12:05 the third night, and it took the fly perfectly. That's my kind of fishing — just looking for that one big fish."

The biggest fish reported during this year's hatch are 25- and 24-inchers taken by Rusty Gates, owner of Gates' Au Sable Lodge and one of the state's premier fly tackle experts. Gates said the biggest fish was cruising in a pool about 1 a.m. and took the fly after an hour of patient and careful casting. During that time Gates often cast his fly perfectly only to watch the monster take a real hex inches away.

"When they're cruising like that, you can't figure out a rhythm to their feeding pattern," Gates said. "You just have to be patient and hope you put the fly in front of the fish at the right time before you spook it."

Hexagenia limbata is America's biggest mayfly, a delicate, 2-inch creature that hatches one night and returns to the river to lay its eggs and die 24 to 48 hours later. Decades ago, locals erroneously tagged it the Michigan caddis. While there's rarely any confusion because the italics are virtually audible when an angler says he intends to fish *THE* caddis hatch.

When the returning spinners are thick on the water, the hatch often triggers a feeding orgy among big, fish-eating trout that normally disdain anything as small as an insect. It's a weird kind of fly fishing in which the angler stands in a night-shrouded river casting not to fish that he sees but those that he hears. But it's addictive, and the sound of big trout slurping down hexes in the dark is one that will never be forgotten.

My job requires a fair amount of travel. Last year I did 50,000 miles on the highways alone. But for the past 10 days I've made every excuse possible to stick around Grayling because the hex hatch came early. The hatch usually starts about June 10 and continues until mid-July. This year, it probably will start to peter out on the main stream by this weekend, but Gates says sporadic hex hatches will continue for three weeks, "and the fish will keep feeding on them. I think it's easier to catch fish when there are fewer flies on the water."

While the main stream and south branch of the Au Sable have the best-known hatches, there is good hex fishing on the Au Sable's north and east branches; the Manistee above CCC Bridge; the Boardman upstream from Traverse City; the Jordan River; parts of the Clam River; the Pere Marquette in the Custer area, and the Black, Pigeon and Sturgeon in the Pigeon River Country State Forest.

There are also hex hatches on many lesser-known streams, and this hatch brings out not just big brown trout but jumbo brookies on smaller waters.

But the most reliable hatches are on the Au Sable, with the Manistee not far behind. This year's unusually warm weather got these big bugs hatching about two weeks ago, popping at night from the mud banks on slow, silty pools where they live in underground burrows. On most rivers, such as the Manistee and north and south branches of the Au Sable, the hexes start hatching in the warmer parts of the water and move upstream over a period of a month.

On the Au Sable mainstream, the hatch usually starts in Grayling and moves downstream because the Au Sable is a topsy-turvy river that gets colder downstream as it is fed by hundreds of cool underground springs.

Because anglers often are on the rivers until the wee hours, many of them miss what is sometimes the best hex fishing of the day, the two hours after dawn when fish are still picking off the occasional spinner that got hung up on a bush or log jam and is finally knocked loose by the current or a gust of wind.

Come to think of it, let the fish keep those hexes undisturbed. Anyone who has been stumbling around in the swift currents of a trout stream until 3 a.m. needs his or her beauty rest.

ERIC SHARP/Detroit Free Press
A trout might mistake this imitation for a Hexagenia limbata, also known as the Michigan caddis.

Do the best flies come in big or small packages?

A continuing argument among fly anglers is how big a fly to use for the hex hatch?

Some popular models look pretty much like the real bugs. Others could moonlight as small birds.

A real Hexagenia limbata has a slender body about 2 inches long, wings about 1½ inches high and two hair-thin, 3-inch tails.

Dan Catau and Rusty Gates prefer flies tied on a No. 8 hook, a 2XL hook that is the same length as a normal No. 4 (the No. 8 has thinner wire and floats better). If a lot of flies are on the water, they might go up to a No. 6.

Sam Surre of Lake Orion is an angler and fly-tyer who believes in the "big fish, big flies" theory. His deer-hair imitations are larger than life, often tied on No. 4 hooks. If there are a lot of flies on the water, he will use an extended body version that's twice as long as the real fly with two sets of wings and hackle to represent two flies floating in tandem.

"If there's a real good hatch, most of the big fish I get take on a down-wing double," he says. "I think the fish recognize that they can get more food for their money."

The bigger the fly, the more calories for the amount of energy they expend to catch it if they can take two flies at a time."

Among the most effective hex flies are Catau's dun and spinner patterns, which seek to present an attractive outline rather than a close imitation. The tail is a white calf tail clump about half as long as the hook (a No. 8, 2XL). The body is yellow wool, and a grizzly hackle is palmered on the abdomen.

In the dun version, a single white calf tail wing is tied in upright, and the fly is finished with a grizzly hackle tied parachute style. For the spinner, white calf wings are tied in spent fashion, one projecting flat on either side of the thorax, and a grizzly hackle is wound conventionally around the body behind and ahead of the wing.

By Eric Sharp

DAN CATAU
DETROIT FREE PRESS
JUNE 21, 1991

BIBLIOGRAPHY

The information contained within this book is a summation of the author's forty years of fly tying and fly-fishing experience. It was not extracted from, nor was it intended to represent, any other publications presently available in the market place. The several publications listed below were only utilized as references to check and add credence to the author's findings.

INDEX OF FLY PATTERNS

ORDER INFORMATION

To order additional copies of *In the Thrill of the Night* forward the following information to:

Brook Trout Press
P. O. Box 738
New Baltimore, Michigan 48047

One copy of *In the Thrill of the Night* costs $15.95 plus $2.50 for shipping and handling.

Number of books requested: _____

Total Enclosed: $_____

Mailing Address:

Name: _____

Address (include zip code):_____

_____

_____

Autograph requests: To _____

Questions? Call Dan Catau at:
(810) 727-8674

Thank you